Stokes Nature Guides

by Donald Stokes

A Guide to Nature in Winter
A Guide to Observing Insect Lives
A Guide to Bird Behavior, Volume I

by Donald and Lillian Stokes

A Guide to Bird Behavior, Volume II
A Guide to Bird Behavior, Volume III
A Guide to Enjoying Wildflowers
A Guide to Animal Tracking and Behavior

by Thomas F. Tyning

A Guide to Amphibians and Reptiles

ALSO BY DONALD STOKES

The Natural History of Wild Shrubs and Vines

ALSO BY DONALD AND LILLIAN STOKES

The Bird Feeder Book
The Hummingbird Book
The Complete Birdhouse Book
The Bluebird Book
The Butterfly Book
The Wildflower Book: East of the Rockies
The Wildflower Book: From the Rockies West

A Guide
to
Bird Behavior

Volume II

A Guide to Bird Behavior

Volume II
In the Wild and at Your Feeder

by Donald W. Stokes and Lillian Q. Stokes

*Illustrated by John Sill,
Deborah Prince,
and Donald Stokes*

Little, Brown and Company
Boston   New York   Toronto   London

Library of Congress Cataloging in Publication Data

Stokes, Donald W.
  A guide to bird behavior.
  Bibliography: p. 323
  Contents: — v. 2. In the wild and at your
feeder.
  1. Birds — Behavior.   I. Stokes, Lillian Q.
II. Title.
[QL698.3.S757 1985]   598.2'51'0973   85-126
ISBN 0-316-81726-0 (hc)
ISBN 0-316-81729-5 (pb)
HC: 10 9 8 7 6 5 4 3 2 1
PB: 10 9 8

Chapter opening illustrations by John Sill,
Copyright © 1983 by John Sill.

Line drawings by Deborah Prince,
Copyright © 1983 by Deborah Prince Smith.

MV

*Published simultaneously in Canada
by Little, Brown & Company (Canada) Limited*

PRINTED IN THE UNITED STATES OF AMERICA

Acknowledgments

THE FIRST AND MOST IMPORTANT ACKNOWLEDGMENT MUST GO TO THE many professional and amateur ornithologists whose careful studies added greatly to our own extensive fieldwork. Their names and works are listed in the bibliography. We would also like to give a special thanks to Betty Porter and Dick Walton for their valuable help in finding nests.

Contents

Behavior-Watching   3
Bird Feeders and Behavior-Watching   11
How to Use This Book   15

Guides to Bird Behavior
  Killdeer   23
  Spotted Sandpiper   37
  Mourning Dove   49
  Belted Kingfisher   61
  Downy Woodpecker   71
  Eastern Phoebe   85
  Eastern Wood Pewee   97
  Barn Swallow   107
  Tufted Titmouse   119
  White-Breasted Nuthatch   131
  Marsh Wren   145
  Brown Thrasher   155
  Wood Thrush   165
  Cedar Waxwing   177
  Yellow Warbler   189
  Eastern Meadowlark   201
  Brown-Headed Cowbird   213

Northern Oriole   225

Scarlet Tanager   237

Northern Cardinal   247

Rose-Breasted Grosbeak   259

Indigo Bunting   271

Rufous-Sided Towhee   283

Chipping Sparrow   295

Field Sparrow   305

Checklist of Nests and Displays   317

Glossary   321

Bibliography   323

A Guide
to
Bird Behavior

Volume II

Behavior-Watching

BIRDS ARE ALWAYS PRESENTING US WITH A WEALTH OF INFORMATION about their lives; however, most of this exciting information goes unnoticed. The difference between receiving or missing it is only a matter of a few minutes of observation, some curiosity, and a little information. The information needed can be found in volumes 1 and 2 of *A Guide to Bird Behavior;* the curiosity and observation can come from you.

For example, on a March morning, a brief walk through our woods just identifying birds would reveal some Cardinals, a Nuthatch, a few Woodpeckers, and a Mourning Dove. But with a little extra time and the information in the guides, this is what we discovered. We started off hearing Cardinal Song from the dense shrubs at the edge of the woods. The clear, whistled notes came from two different locations, one Song alternating with the other. We knew that both male and female Cardinals sing and that when birds of the same sex alternate Songs it is a territorial interaction, but when birds of different sexes alternate Songs it is courtship. We searched for the birds and found that they were male and female. This was a good sign that the two had paired and that in the coming months we would see their lovely courtship feeding and nest-building somewhere in this vicinity.

In the same area, we heard a White-breasted Nuthatch giving a call like "werwerwerwer." This is the Nuthatch Song and is given only by the male. We located the bird at the top of an old oak and saw the curious bowing action that goes along with Song. We knew that the female often approaches the male while he is singing, so we waited. Soon we heard the Ank-call, which alerted us to the presence of the female. After she landed near the male, he stopped singing and the two started moving up and down the tree in their "mechanical toy" fashion, feeding and giving their soft Ip-calls to stay in contact. Clearly, the two were closely associated, and we knew that within the next few weeks we could look forward to seeing courtship behavior, in which the male brings food to the female.

As we walked into more open woods, we heard loud, very rapid pecking from a Woodpecker. We knew this to be Drumming and that its function is like that of Song in other birds. We looked for the bird and saw that it was a Downy Woodpecker, and because it lacked red on the back of its head, we knew it was a female. Suddenly two males flew into view chasing each other and giving excited Queek-queek-calls. This is a typical interaction early in the season indicating that the female is probably paired with one of the males and the other male is competing for her. Even though we didn't wait for the end of the chasing, we knew that we were in the pair's territory and would probably hear the female Drum from that same spot at other times in the coming weeks.

As we started back, we heard a Mourning Dove cooing in the distance. Mourning Doves have two different versions of cooing, one long and one short. We recognized this to be the Short-coo, an exciting discovery, for at this time of year the call is usually given by the male dove to attract his mate to a potential nest site. Even though we didn't see the bird, we knew that in the next week or two we should be on the lookout for nest-building in the area.

This is just a brief example of the information birds are giving us all the time. For most bird-watchers, our walk would yield "just Cardinals, Nuthatches, Downy Woodpeckers, and a Mourning Dove"; but for the behavior-watcher, it clearly offers a great deal more. It provides a unique look into the inner lives of the birds and sets the stage for future walks by suggesting what might be looked for in the weeks ahead.

After publication of the first volume of *A Guide to Bird Behavior*, many people expressed their thanks for a new approach to bird-watching, one that stressed observing what birds do rather than simply identifying them and walking on. But at the same time, they said that many of their favorite birds were not included. Because of this, we have written a second volume, including twenty-five more birds. As in the first volume, we have chosen birds that are common, accessible, and whose breeding range includes the greater portion of the United States and southern Canada. The birds chosen for the first volume were those whose behavior is most easily seen, either because the birds are extremely common or because they are conspicuous and live in open areas. Most of the birds in the second volume are just as common and easily observed. But a few birds in volume 2 can be more secretive or live in less accessible habitats and are therefore slightly more challenging to the behavior-watcher.

The behavior of birds can be divided into two broad categories: maintenance behavior and social behavior. The former includes all actions a bird does to maintain itself, such as preening, feeding, bathing, and so on (see the Summary of Maintenance Behavior later in this chapter). The latter includes all interactions between birds, such as courtship, territoriality, breeding, flocking. This guide deals primarily with social behavior, for this is one of the most exciting aspects of birds and one that has often been neglected. In social behavior, one individual is coordinating its life and actions with those of another, and this always involves communication of some kind, either in fixed sounds or gestures or in general movement patterns. This struggle to connect separate lives is common to all animal life, and we find that through watching it in birds we have become more aware of its importance in the lives of all animals.

This application of behavior-watching is one of its deepest rewards, but at the same time it is one of its most common pitfalls; for although behavior-watching can produce insights into human behavior, applying human motives to birds can be very limiting. When most of us try to supply motives for the behavior of animals, we invariably use motives that we would have in the same situation. "The bird scolded me." "The mother bird was teaching its young how to fly." "He sang happily from his perch." All of these statements are anthropomorphic: they are assumptions about the motives of birds based on human values. This tendency to explain the actions of birds in human terms greatly limits our ability to learn new things about the avian world. It is like searching the bottom of a pond for plants and animals and never getting past our own image on the water's surface.

What a bird does and why it does it are two different things. One is based on observation and is therefore mostly fact; the other is based on assumption and so is mostly speculation. The problem is that we have a strong tendency to mix the two, confusing facts with assumptions. In your own observations, keep descriptions of behavior and conclusions about the meaning of the behavior separate. If you do this, your observations will be of greater value to yourself and to other behavior-watchers.

Behavior-watching is simply observing what birds do. Its two most important ingredients are time and curiosity. The time needed is only two or three minutes, and the curiosity can be as simple as asking "What is this bird doing and why?" If you can spend these extra minutes with a bird and ask this question, then you are on your way to being a seasoned behavior-watcher.

No special equipment is needed to behavior-watch; however, a pair of binoculars are useful, for they enable you to get a closer look at behavior while watching from a distance so as not to disturb the bird. You may also want to bring along an identification guide, although this is not a necessity, since you can start behavior-watching whether or not you know the name of the bird.

When we go out behavior-watching, we start looking and listening as soon as we get out the door, whether in the city or the country, because fascinating behavior can happen anywhere. We listen for all bird sounds and keep our eyes open for all interactions — those are the main indicators of social behavior.

If we see an interaction, we try to answer the following questions about it: What species is/are interacting? What happens before, during, and after the interaction? How long does it last? Is it repeated? Is it conspicuous or hard to see? How many birds are involved? Are all birds in the interaction behaving alike?

Often when birds are interacting, they make sounds or assume unusual positions with their bodies and/or feathers. These auditory or visual displays are part of the birds' language. They are among the most exciting and important aspects of bird behavior, and learning to recognize them is essential to understanding the interactions of birds. When we see what we believe to be a display, we try to answer these questions: What species is displaying? How many different displays is it using? How will I distinguish between the different displays of one bird? How long does the display last? What does the bird do before, during, and after the display? Do other birds or other animals seem to respond to the display? Does the display include both gestures and sounds? In all cases, it is also helpful to observe whether the bird is male or female, young or adult.

As well as observing specific behavior, we always take a general, overall impression of the bird we are watching. Is it alone, in a pair, small flock, or large flock? Is it conspicuous or secretive? Is its display repertoire large or small? Over the months, a simple record of these features will add up to a great deal of information about the behavior of each bird.

The social behavior of most birds is periodic, so it is often productive to be patient and wait through periods of inactivity. It is also important to be aware of how your own presence is affecting the birds you are watching. In most cases you will want to stay far enough away so that you don't disturb their natural patterns, but at other times you may want to be closer and see how the birds respond. The majority of social behavior occurs from sunrise until about 11:00 A.M. and then again from about 3:00 P.M. until sunset. At midday, birds are generally quiet and hard to locate.

During your behavior-watching you are bound to find nests. Nests are ideal places to watch behavior and are obviously of the utmost importance to the bird's successful breeding. Because of this, care must be taken not to disturb the birds or the nest when it is being actively used. Always observe the nest from far enough away that you do not disturb the bird's normal activities. You can approach the nest for a closer look, but do so when the birds are away, make your visit brief, and be careful not to harm the vegetation around the nest. If nests are over your head, a small pocket mirror on a pole will enable you to see into them. Do not visit the nest more than once a day, and remember that the less you visit it, the greater the bird's chances of having a successful brood. One final note: many birds have no better than a 50 percent success rate for nests, so if you have been careful in your visits, don't blame yourself for the failure of a given nest.

These suggestions are only guidelines for your own explorations. Some of you will find that just watching bird behavior and using this guide to help interpret what you see will be enough. Others may want to make careful records of their observations and not only discover all they can about the birds in this guide, but continue learning about other species as well.

The most important thing to remember in all of this is that the discovery of bird behavior is open to all. The general public believes that all of the common aspects of nature are already well known. Nothing could be further from the truth in the field of bird behavior. In fact, in most cases there has not been enough observation to know for sure what is individual behavior and what is the general behavior of the species. Because of this, what you see birds do is very important. Do not discount it; remember it and record it. One of the main purposes of this guide is to encourage everybody to participate in helping to discover the behavior of our common birds. If just a fraction of the energy that now goes into bird-watching were to go into behavior-watching, within a very short time our knowledge about the behavior of our common birds would be greatly increased.

SUMMARY OF MAINTENANCE BEHAVIOR

Maintenance behavior includes all things that a bird does to take care of its own body. Much of maintenance behavior is very similar in all species; for example, there is not much difference in the way the various birds in this volume sleep, preen, and bathe. Because of this, we have not included maintenance behavior in the individual chapters, but rather present a summary of its main types. The information here can be applied to most of the species in this guide.

Eating

Eating is the most common maintenance behavior of birds. Each species of bird is uniquely designed to take advantage of a particular source of food. The bill, feet, feathers, and eyes are all adapted to aid the bird in gathering and breaking apart food. It is fun to observe how the differences in the shapes of birds' bills reflect what they eat. Hooked bills are for tearing flesh, conical bills are often for breaking seed husks, fine bills are for eating insects, long bills are for probing into mud, and so on. After getting familiar with which shapes go with which food, you will find that you can look at a new bird and guess what it eats, simply by looking at its bill.

Sleeping

Many people wonder where birds go at night. In general, they go to as secure and protected a place as they can find. Most land birds roost in a sheltered part of a tree, bush, or brush pile. Some even roost in tall grass on the ground or in marshes. Safety for others, such as waterfowl, may mean sleeping together in the center of a lake or pond, out of the reach of a fox or other land predator. Hole-nesting birds, such as Woodpeckers or Nuthatches, spend the nights in tree holes, especially in winter. When birds go to sleep, they fluff up their feathers and frequently tuck their head back behind a shoulder.

Preening

Feather condition is of the utmost importance to the health and safety of a bird. Feathers are incredibly strong yet light structures that keep birds warm and dry. Birds preen their feathers by running them through their bills. They also coat their feathers with oil that they get from a special gland on their backs at the base of their tail. They apply the oil by getting it on their bill and then rubbing it off on their feathers.

Bathing

Birds take baths in dust or water to help maintain their feathers. Dust bathing may help remove parasites from the birds' plumage. After a rain, birds often use puddles to bathe in.

Anting

Anting is a maintenance behavior in which birds squeeze ants in their bills and rub the juice on their feathers; or they place the ants on their body and let them momentarily crawl through their feathers. The function of anting is not fully known, but a chemical in ants called formic acid is thought to destroy feather mites and thus may help the bird to protect its plumage.

Sunbathing

Birds sunbathe by ruffling their feathers, spreading their wings and tail, and crouching down in a warm, sunny place. Sunbathing usually lasts for only a few minutes. Nobody knows exactly why birds sunbathe. Two possible explanations are that the rays of the sun help the bird produce vitamin D or that sunlight is somehow soothing to the bird's skin during molting.

Bird Feeders and Behavior-Watching

ONE OF THE BEST WAYS OF BEHAVIOR-WATCHING IS TO ATTRACT BIRDS to your house. By establishing feeders and feeding stations, you will be provided with endless opportunities to see birds communicate with one another. Not only will you see behavior and begin to understand its meaning at your feeders, you will also have attracted birds to your property and therefore increased the chances that they will remain and possibly nest in your area during spring and summer. Some of our best behavior-watching moments have taken place right outside our window.

SETTING UP BIRD FEEDERS

The best way to begin, in our experience, is with three types of feeders:

1. A hanging cylindrical feeder filled with sunflower seeds. Sunflower seeds are highly attractive to a large variety of birds. Hulled sunflower seeds, which are available through some seed companies, are even more attractive. Do not use mixed seed in these feeders, for the birds will only pick out the sunflower seeds and scatter the rest on the ground.

2. An area of cleared ground with cracked corn and mixed seed scattered over it. This is inexpensive and attracts a lot of species that will only feed on the ground. If you have some shrubs or brush at the edge of this feeding station, the birds will like it even more.

3. A hanging bag of suet. This attracts Woodpeckers especially and will also be used by some species that are attracted to your sunflower feeder. You can also drill one-inch-diameter holes in a small log, hammer the suet into the holes, and suspend the log from a branch.

Other ways to attract birds to your backyard include thistle-seed feeders, fruit feeders, birdbaths, birdhouses, and shrub plantings. An excellent reference in this regard is *The New Handbook of Attracting Birds* by Thomas P. McElroy, Jr.

BEHAVIOR AT YOUR FEEDER

For the birds in this volume that regularly come to feeders, we have included a section called Feeder Behavior at the end of their Behavior Descriptions. In addition to these descriptions of specific behavior, we would like to give you some general guidelines for interpreting the behavior of all birds at feeders.

First of all, it is important to remember that a bird feeder is unlike anything the birds encounter in the wild — it is an inexhaustible and highly concentrated source of food. Because of this, it attracts more birds to a smaller space than would normally occur, and this, in turn, increases competition and aggression between the birds. Therefore, most of the interactions occurring at feeders are aggressive.

Very few animals engage in outright fighting when competing over food. Most have evolved displays to settle disputes because displays take less energy and involve less risk than fighting. There are four aggressive displays commonly used by feeder birds, and being able to recognize them will greatly add to your enjoyment and understanding of what occurs at your feeder.

One of the most common displays, Crest-raise, involves raising the feathers on the top of the head. It is not only given by birds with obvious crests, such as Titmice, Cardinals, and some Jays, but also by most other songbirds (passerines). On birds without crests, such as Goldfinches, Sparrows, and Woodpeckers, Crest-raise is more subtle and merely alters the outline of the head, making it slightly more pointed on top or square at the back. You can also recognize the display on these birds by seeing the feather tips at the back of the head, where the feathers are most raised. Crest-raise usually lasts only a second or two and occurs immediately after two birds land near each other.

Normal posture   Crest-raise display

Another subtle display is called Wing-droop. This is very common, so much so that some birds in your identification guides are pictured in this display. Normally, birds' wings fold over the top of the base of their tail. In Wing-droop, the tail is slightly raised and the wingtips are lowered, making them appear to be points below the tail. The wingtips can be drooped to varying degrees depending on the intensity of the display. Wing-droop tends to be held for several seconds and is usually given by the more aggressive bird in an interaction.

Normal posture   Wing-droop
display

A third display is Head-forward, in which the bird assumes a horizontal posture with its bill pointing straight forward at another bird. Sometimes the bill is gaped (open). This is usually done for only a second or two. The displaying bird looks as if it is about to peck its opponent, and in fact this may be the origin of the display.

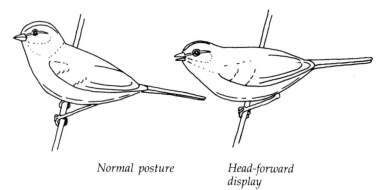

Normal posture   Head-forward
                      display

A fourth aggressive behavior is Perch-taking, in which one bird flies at and takes the perch of another bird. Perch-taking is extremely common, and although it is not exactly a display, it is an expression of dominance, the dominant bird being the one that takes the perch and makes the other bird leave. It is very common at feeders.

Look for these displays whenever you see two birds land near each other at your feeder or whenever you hear the short, harsh sounds like "chip" or "chek" that often accompany them. Also, look closely at birds' normal feather and body positions. Having a clear sense of those enables you to recognize quickly when there is a change in the crest, wingtips, or posture.

How to Use This Book

THE INFORMATION ON EACH BIRD IN THIS GUIDE IS ORGANIZED INTO three sections: a behavior calendar, a display guide, and behavior descriptions.

The behavior descriptions form the main body of information. They describe in detail six major areas of each bird's behavior: territory, courtship, nest-building, breeding, plumage, and seasonal movement. Additional sections on flock behavior and feeder behavior are included for those species that have significant behavior in these categories.

Preceding each bird's behavior descriptions are two short references: the behavior calendar and the display guide. The behavior calendar tells you when in the year the major types of a bird's behavior take place. The display guide provides pictures and descriptions for field identification of the main displays used by each species. Both of these short guides will refer you to sections of the behavior descriptions for further information on what you have seen.

The guide is designed to help you interpret what you see in the field. For example, you hear a Mourning Dove continually giving a short version of its cooing call in early March. To find out what is happening, you could do either of two things. One would be to turn to the display guide and look up the call under auditory displays; you would find it named the Short-coo. Following a description of the display is a reference to a section of the behavior descriptions where you would find further information on the meaning of the display. The other approach would be to look at the

Mourning Dove behavior calendar and see what types of behavior the birds do in March. You could then read the appropriate behavior descriptions and locate the behavior that you observed.

Besides using the guide in the field, you may want to consult it before going out to familiarize yourself with the behavior of several birds that you know you will be able to observe. Read at least the introduction to each bird. If you have more time, read the behavior descriptions that are appropriate for that month and get to know the distinctions among the various displays.

Not all aspects of a bird's behavior can be learned in one reading or one session of behavior-watching. More likely, you will alternate between observing in the field and reading in the guide, each time learning a little more about the bird's behavior. A glossary is provided at the end of the book to help explain any unfamiliar terms.

If the birds in this guide are not already familiar to you, the drawings at the beginning of each chapter will help you to identify them. For expert field identification of these and other birds, the best book to have is *Birds of North America* by Chandler S. Robbins, Bertel Bruun, and Herbert S. Zim.

Below are detailed descriptions of each section.

BEHAVIOR CALENDAR

The behavior calendar is only an approximation of the timing of the bird's life cycle and is meant to give the observer a rough idea of when the behaviors described are most common. Clearly, timing varies widely within North America. Because of this, the behavior calendar has been calculated for the middle latitudes of the continent (around forty degrees latitude, or, roughly, along a line drawn from Philadelphia, through Indianapolis and Denver, to slightly above San Francisco).

It has been found that breeding times vary ten to fifteen days for each change of five degrees latitude. Therefore, with the aid of the map below, you can quickly become accustomed to adjusting the behavior calendar for whatever area of the continent you are in. As you continue to observe behavior patterns, you may want to record a more accurate estimate of their timing for your particular area.

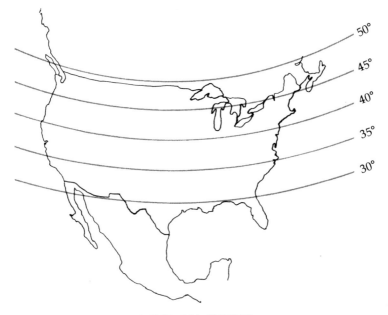

DISPLAY GUIDE

The display guide lists the major displays used by each species. A display is a gesture or sound a bird makes that, when used in certain situations, affects the behavior of other animals near the bird. More loosely, it is a signal birds use to communicate with each other.

Bird displays are generally divided into two groups: those that are heard (auditory displays) and those that are seen (visual displays). Visual displays have been illustrated in those cases where a picture is particularly helpful, and the auditory displays have been represented with verbal approximations whenever feasible. When a call usually accompanies a visual display, it is listed below it. When no call is listed, the display is usually accomplished in silence.

The verbal approximations of the calls have been punctuated in four different ways to show the timing of the sounds:

tseetseetseetsee — spoken continuously with no pause
tsee tsee tsee — slight pause
tseet, tseet, — moderate pause
tseet. tseet. — substantial pause

The descriptions of the auditory displays are not sufficiently detailed to enable you to distinguish the calls of one species from those of another. But this is not as important for behavior-watching as is being able to distinguish the different calls of the same species. For this purpose the display guide will be extremely helpful. After most of the displays, you will see a reference to one or more sections of the behavior descriptions, such as "*See* Territory, Courtship." By reading these sections, you will understand more fully the use and context of the display. Displays that are used throughout the year may have no reference to specific sections of the behavior descriptions.

The seasons in which each display is commonly given are listed with the display and represented by symbols: Sp — spring, Su — summer, F — fall, and W — winter.

BEHAVIOR DESCRIPTIONS

Territory

Territory has been defined as "any defended area." It is important to remember that territory is not the same for all birds; it is extremely varied. Territory is categorized into various types, depending on what occurs in it. Some territories include only the nest and the two or three feet of space around it; other territories include a larger area for mating and/or feeding.

Courtship

In this guide, courtship refers to pair formation, pair maintenance, and mating. Pair formation includes the initial contacts between a male and female of the same species, both in breeding condition. Often, after a pair of birds are committed to each other, they may continue to perform displays when they meet or they may have extended periods of mate-feeding. This is pair maintenance, or the sustaining of the relationship and commitment between the two birds.

Mating is used here to refer to copulation as well as the displays that come before and after it. Copulation is similar in all common birds. The female usually tilts forward and raises her tail feathers, while the male steps onto her back and lowers his tail feathers to make contact with her. In the case of most birds, copulation lasts for only a few seconds but may be repeated many times. The displays surrounding copulation are often some of the most elaborate in the birds' repertoire.

Nest-Building

This section offers a guide to locating the nest of each species. To those of you who have not done it before, this may seem an impossible task, but with the help of the behavioral clues to the nest location, you will find it easier than you expect. With some species, finding the nest is essential for you to see the most interesting elements of the birds' behavior.

Breeding

This is the period from the beginning of egg-laying until the time when the young are independent. It is divided into three phases: egg-laying and incubation; the nestling phase; and the fledgling phase. The nestling phase is from the time the young hatch until they leave the nest. The fledgling phase lasts from the time they leave the nest until they are no longer dependent upon the parents for food.

Plumage

Though plumage is not an aspect of the birds' social behavior, it is helpful when watching behavior to know when the molting periods occur and how the birds' appearance changes through the year. This section also gives clues that help in distinguishing the sexes, by physical appearance as well as behavior.

Seasonal Movement

This section describes the large-scale movements of birds that regularly occur each year. The largest seasonal movement of most birds is migration, but nonmigratory as well as migratory birds often shift slightly from one environment or area to another, and I have described these lesser movements where significant.

For only a few species in this guide is migration a clear-cut phenomenon — birds flying south in the fall and north in the spring. For the majority of birds in this guide, migration patterns vary within a species, some members migrating long distances, others migrating short distances, and still others remaining as year-round residents. Some birds even migrate one year and stay put the next. The problems of studying migration are immense, with the result that there is still very little known about this aspect of our common birds.

Flock Behavior

This type of behavior usually occurs in fall and winter and involves flocks of one or more species that coordinate their actions in some way. Often there is a social structure of the flock, such as a hierarchy, which can be seen by following the interactions between individuals.

Feeder Behavior

Home bird feeders are an ideal place to observe and learn about bird behavior. A Feeder Behavior section has been provided for those birds that regularly visit feeders. In each are described the bird's favorite foods, its general behavior at the feeder, its most common displays given in feeder situations, and other behavior that you may see in the vicinity of the feeder. Reading the Feeder Behavior sections of this guide is probably the best way to begin your study of bird behavior, especially if you are starting in fall and winter, when most birds are attracted to feeders.

Killdeer / *Charadrius vociferus*

THE KILLDEER'S SCIENTIFIC NAME, *VOCIFERUS*, IS WELL CHOSEN SINCE this bird spends long stretches of its breeding period giving its Kideah-calls. The calls are so plaintive and distressing in quality that people hearing them for the first time often think the bird is wounded. Early breeding activity is particularly noisy, for when two males are calling and chasing each other over a territory, neighboring birds often are attracted and join in the displaying. This can easily continue for a whole afternoon and then be resumed the next day.

Once a pair settle down in a territory, the behavior-watcher has a real challenge: locating the nest. The nest is only a shallow scrape in some bare earth. The eggs are speckled and blend so well with the ground that you can be standing right over the nest and still not see it. Luckily, the birds will give you a few clues to the nest's location. When you come near a nest with eggs, they are sure to do their distraction display to lead you away from the site. In this display they call piteously and drag their wing and tail along the ground. If you move away from the area and are patient, one of the birds will cautiously return to the nest and resume sitting on the eggs.

Juvenal Killdeers are attractive little balls of down and well worth the effort of watching a nest daily until the eggs hatch. A day or two before they hatch, you can see cracks in the eggs and, if you put your head near, hear the young peeping. Soon after they hatch they can walk and feed themselves, and the parents will lead them away from the nest to open areas where the family will feed together.

BEHAVIOR CALENDAR

	TERRITORY	COURTSHIP	NEST-BUILDING	BREEDING	PLUMAGE	SEASONAL MOVEMENT	FLOCK BEHAVIOR
JANUARY							
FEBRUARY					■		
MARCH	■	■			■	■	
APRIL	■	■	■	■	■		
MAY	■	■	■	■			
JUNE	■	■	■	■			
JULY	■	■		■	■		■
AUGUST				■	■	■	■
SEPTEMBER					■	■	
OCTOBER					■	■	
NOVEMBER							
DECEMBER							

DISPLAY GUIDE

Visual Displays

Circling-Flights
Male or Female   *Sp*
Bird flies in a circle up to a half-mile in diameter (usually smaller), sometimes rising out of sight. Often uses a distinctive wingbeat that is deeper and slower than that used in normal flight. Can last from several minutes to over an hour.

CALL Kideah-calls

CONTEXT Done mostly by males soon after they arrive on the breeding ground. Often interspersed with giving the Kideah-call from the ground. Occasionally done at night. *See* Territory, Courtship

Horizontal-Run
Male or Female   *Sp Su*
Bird assumes a horizontal posture and makes short runs at another bird. Back feathers may be slightly ruffled and tail may be spread.

CALL Stutter-call or Kideah-calls

CONTEXT Given during aggressive encounters, the more dominant bird usually doing the display. A similar display by the male may precede copulation. *See* Territory, Courtship

Collar-Show
Male or Female   *Sp Su*
Bird lifts head and extends neck, exposing more and more of its black collars. Especially the collar nearest the bill widens noticeably.

CALL None

CONTEXT A subtle display given in feeding areas and territories by more dominant birds. *See* Territory

Scraping

Male or Female   *Sp Su*

With neck extended, the body is tipped forward so that breast is near ground. Often accompanied by a backward kicking of the legs that may create a scraped-out depression. Tail may be raised and spread or flipped back and forth. Occasionally bird interrupts display with moments of tossing pebbles and debris over its back.

CALL None or Kideah-calls

CONTEXT Occurs during advertising by males early in the season, during aggressive encounters on the territory, as a precopulatory display, and during nest-building. *See* Territory, Courtship, Nest-building

Side-Tilt

Male or Female   *Sp Su*

Bird runs a short distance, stops, and tilts to one side. Wing on that side is drooped and tail is spread, exposing bright orange rump. A more intense version is done as the distraction or "broken-wing" display. In this the bird may flutter one or both wings and during runs may hold both wings out to the side and drooped.

CALL Stutter-call or Kideah-calls

CONTEXT Done by birds being chased by other Killdeers. When bird is closely chased, Side-tilts become more frequent.

Occasionally the displaying bird may fly back at chaser. Also done as a distraction display to potential predators near the nest or young. *See* Territory, Breeding

Bobbing

Male or Female   *Sp Su*

A rapid lifting and lowering of the head
CALL None
CONTEXT Given in situations of mild alarm

Auditory Displays

The auditory displays are difficult to interpret because they are so varied. In the same situation a number of different calls and their variations may be given. Two calls are fairly distinct; these are the Pup-call and Stuttering-call. The rest have been grouped under Kideah-calls.

Kideah-Calls

Male or Female   *Sp Su F*

TYPE 1 A single plaintive note, either ascending "deyeet" or descending "deah." Usually repeated many times
TYPE 2 A two-part call sounding like "killdeah"
TYPE 3 Three or more part calls like "kitadeah" or "k'k'k'k'deer"
CONTEXT Given in a variety of contexts, such as aggressive encounters, alarm, courtship, and territory advertisement. *See* Territory, Courtship

Stutter-Call

Male or Female   *Sp Su*

t't't't't't   A rapid series of short syllables that sound like a stuttering trill

CONTEXT Given during aggressive encounters, alarm, and courtship. *See* Courtship

Pup-Pup-Call

Male or Female   *Sp Su*

A short, clucking syllable repeated several times at a moderate rate. Very distinct from the Kideah-calls and Stutter-call.

CONTEXT Given by members of the pair, usually near the nest. At times may be used near fledglings in order to gather them together. *See* Breeding

BEHAVIOR DESCRIPTIONS

Territory

Type: Mating, nesting
Size: An acre or less
Main behavior: Kideah-calls, Circling-flights, chases
Duration of defense: From the arrival of the males until the end of breeding

When the males first arrive on the breeding ground they may just feed together in small groups and not start territory formation immediately. Even after territories have been formed, the birds often share a feeding area at some other location with other Killdeers. At these communal feeding areas the only displays are Collar-show and Horizontal-run, and these are used to express temporary dominance over a particular part of the feeding area.

Wherever Killdeers decide to form territories, there is bound to be a great deal of displaying and interaction. Territories are generally located in open areas with sparse vegetation, including such places as lake shores, cultivated fields, waste spaces, playing fields, and gravel rooftops. Territories are usually widely dispersed, but Killdeers are often attracted by the conflicts of other Killdeers and join them in displaying. This often creates scenes with four or five birds all interacting, sometimes for long periods.

Male Killdeers usually return to their territories of previous years and arrive there before the females. A male on his territory may do several displays. One is to stand on a prominent place and repeatedly give Kideah-calls, most often of type 1 or 2. While doing this he may tilt his head up to the sky, possibly looking for other Killdeers. At other times he may do small Circling-flights over the territory, giving Kideah-calls of any type. These two displays may be given to advertise the bird's presence to females and other males. A third activity is Scraping, which he may do in several areas of the territory.

When other Killdeers arrive, he is likely to do more Scraping or join them in Circling-flights accompanied by continuous Kideah-calls. If two or more birds meet on the ground, they may engage in chases, with the more dominant bird doing the Horizontal-run display. During pauses in the chase, one or more birds may do Collar-show. Occasionally, a chased bird may do Side-tilt. At the border of a territory, two birds may engage in Horizontal-run parallel to each other, their path following roughly the border of the territory. These interactions can continue for an hour or more.

Defense of the territory continues into the fledgling phase but is then usually stopped, as several families may join together in good feeding areas.

Courtship

Main behavior: Scraping, copulation
Duration: From pair formation until incubation

The male seems to have a variety of responses to the female when she first arrives on the territory. In some cases he seems to treat her as he would an intruding male, with chases, Horizontal-runs, and Circling-flights. As the female remains on the territory instead of fleeing, the male's aggressive displays lessen and he finally accepts her presence. In other cases, females seem able to enter a male's territory and join with him with very little aggression on the part of the male.

Once two birds are paired, they defend the territory and stay close together during most of the day. Their other main activities before egg-laying are Scraping and copulation. During Scraping, both birds approach a spot and start doing the display together, tipping forward and kicking back with their feet. During this display, they may both toss bits of stones or grass over their backs. These Scraping bouts may be repeated at several spots on the territory. Following Scraping, both birds preen and feed or they may start doing the displays that precede copulation.

In copulation, the male approaches the female, sometimes in the Horizontal-run. Once beside her, both he and she may stamp their feet up and down. Then the male steps onto the back of the female and continues to stamp his feet. Suddenly he bends his tail down to make contact. Then he gets off her back. If the birds do not repeat copulation they are both likely to fly off. Calls during these displays include the Stutter-call and various Kideah-calls. Copulation may be repeated three to four times a day in the period just before egg-laying and it may continue to occur even into incubation.

Copulation and Scraping take place only on the territory.

Nest-Building

Placement: On ground in open areas with sparse vegetation
Size: Inside diameter 2–4 inches; inside depth 1–1½ inches
Materials: A slight depression in the ground, may be lined with a variety
of materials, such as pebbles, woodchips, grasses, and other debris

Bouts of Scraping during courtship result in a number of saucer-like depressions in the ground. To one of these the female will add a few small pebbles and bits of debris, and that is the extent of nest-building. This minimal change in the environment results in a nest that is well camouflaged. Added to this is the fact that the eggs are mottled just like the stones and earth surrounding the nest, so that even when you know where a nest is, it can be difficult to locate it again.

Locating the Nest

WHERE TO LOOK In open areas, bare of vegetation and often containing pebbles or rocks. Can be in unusual or unexpected locations, such as on rooftops, between railroad ties, in dumps, or on playing fields.

WHEN TO LOOK From a few days after the birds arrive until midsummer

1. Two or more Killdeers are displaying on the territory.

2. Killdeers are sneaky about their nest location. When disturbed, they leave the nest quietly and then crouch down in other places as if incubating.

3. At other times the birds will lead you away from the nest while doing their distraction display.

Breeding

Eggs: 3–5, usually 4. Light brown with irregular black and brown spots
Incubation: 24–28 days, by both male and female
Nestling phase: A few hours to none
Fledgling phase: About 5 weeks
Broods: 1–2

Egg-Laying and Incubation

Eggs are usually laid one per day until the clutch is complete. Incubation, which is done by both male and female, starts after the last egg is laid. While one bird incubates, the other usually remains nearby, but occasionally it may leave the territory to feed in another area. Attentive periods range from fifty to ninety minutes, and during that time the bird may incubate, turn the eggs to keep them evenly warm, move pebbles around the edge of the nest, or on hot days stand above the eggs to shade them.

Several displays may be seen when the birds exchange places on the nest. The arriving bird may call and the incubating bird flutter its wings and give Kideah-calls or Pup-pup-calls. Then the arriving bird will walk toward the nest and possibly even nudge the incubator off, or both birds may meet away from the nest and copulate. Other exchanges at the nest may involve no displays at all.

If you approach the nest during this stage you are almost sure to see the version of the Side-tilt that is used as a distraction display. One or both birds will immediately move away from the area of the nest and flutter along the ground, leaning to one side, spreading the tail, and giving piteous cries. With these displays they will continuously try to lead you away from the nest site. Once you back up far enough from the nest, the birds will stop displaying and cautiously return. Amazingly, the birds are rarely bothered by cars, and if you approach them by car or return to your car to watch, they will go about their normal activities.

Audible "chips" can be heard from within the eggs eighteen to forty-eight hours before hatching if you put your ear very near them. And pipping (breaking of the shell) of the eggs starts eighteen to thirty-six hours before hatching. Hatching may occur over four to sixteen hours, and once the shells are broken, the adults immediately pick up the pieces and fly off with them, dropping them in another area away from the nest.

In northern locations, Killdeers may start egg-laying early in the season and then get caught in a cold spell or even in snow. These eggs and nests are abandoned, and egg-laying is then repeated in another area of the territory when the cold and snow have gone.

Nestling Phase
There is basically no nestling phase for Killdeers, since the young are precocial — they can walk and feed themselves right after hatching. Sometimes the young are brooded several hours after hatching but then soon leave the nest, never to return.

Fledgling Phase
Once the chicks have hatched, the parents lead them gradually to areas with abundant food and some cover. This may or may not be in the nesting territory. If it is outside the original territory, the parents may defend both areas, the initial territory being needed for any possible renestings. On the first day, the chicks may move up to one hundred twenty feet from the nest, and then they will continue to move as is necessary on following days. Brooding by one or both parents occurs frequently during the first few days and, of course, during the nights. This tapers off until the young are brooded only in the cool morning and evening hours or during showers. When the young become dispersed, the adults gather

them by giving the Pup-pup-call, which the young answer with faint peep-peep calls; thus parents and young locate each other. After the first week or two of this fledgling phase, the parents are more likely to circle over and fly at predators than do the distraction display. The chicks are always attended by the parents except when the parents are engaged with a predator or involved with copulation leading to a second brood. If there is a second brood, the female incubates the eggs while the male watches over the young of the first brood.

Plumage

DISTINGUISHING THE SEXES There is no way to distinguish male from female through plumage, and even through behavior the only sure way is to see the birds copulating.

DISTINGUISHING JUVENALS FROM ADULTS The juvenals are very similar to adults except that their upper feathers are margined with lighter edges, their dark neck bands are narrower and often gray or brown instead of black.

MOLTS Killdeers undergo two molts per year. From July to November they have a complete molt of all feathers, and from February to June they have a partial molt of primarily their body feathers and not their wing or tail feathers.

Seasonal Movement

During fall, Killdeers travel by day in small groups, often so high that you wouldn't know they were going over if it weren't for their Kideah-calls, which can be heard from the ground. They travel as far as South America and may at times be mixed with other shorebirds, such as Yellowlegs, Turnstones, Plovers, and Sandpipers.

Migration north starts in March and the birds usually arrive singly on their breeding grounds.

Flock Behavior

In July and August, flocks of Killdeers gather on mudflats where there is adequate food. In some cases the birds are aggressive to each other and repeatedly use the Horizontal-run and Stutter-call. It appears as if the birds are defending temporary feeding sites before leaving on migration.

Spotted Sandpiper / *Actitis macularia*

MANY PEOPLE HAVE PROBABLY NEVER HEARD OF THE SPOTTED SAND-piper, let alone seen it, and yet it is common and breeds all across the northern half of North America. It is probably unknown because it lives along the unpopulated shores of lakes and streams. In these areas, only fishermen are sure to have seen it flutter across the water with its characteristic stiff, shallow wingbeats. It is one of our few sandpipers whose breeding behavior can be seen, for most of the others spend the summer in the far north and Arctic.

The Spotted Sandpiper reverses the usual roles of the sexes in birds' lives. The female is the first to arrive and the one who displays and fights with other females to define and defend a territory. When the males arrive, she is also the one to take the lead in courtship and does the majority of the displaying. After the nest is made and the eggs laid, the female in many cases leaves to let the male do all of the incubating and caring for the young.

Not only are the sex roles reversed, but in a majority of cases Spotted Sandpipers are polygamous, or more specifically, polyan-drous, the female having two or more males as mates. When she has more than one mate, she courts the male, lays a clutch of eggs for him to incubate and raise, and immediately leaves him to court another male. Up to four or five males have been reported for one female.

The auditory displays of the Spotted Sandpiper are another interesting feature of its behavior. Rather than having many distinct calls, it has a continuum of variations between two versions of its Song. One version of Song seems to be associated with aggression and the other with courtship. The variations in between probably have meanings of their own as well.

BEHAVIOR CALENDAR

	TERRITORY	COURTSHIP	NEST-BUILDING	BREEDING	PLUMAGE	SEASONAL MOVEMENT	FLOCK BEHAVIOR
JANUARY							■
FEBRUARY							■
MARCH					■		
APRIL	■				■	■	
MAY	■	■	■	■		■	
JUNE	■	■	■	■			
JULY	■	■		■			
AUGUST				■	■		■
SEPTEMBER					■	■	■
OCTOBER						■	■
NOVEMBER							■
DECEMBER							■

DISPLAY GUIDE

Visual Displays

Strutting

Female   *Sp Su*

With neck extended, throat feathers ruffled, wings drooped, and tail lowered and spread, the bird struts in a prominent place, such as on a fallen log. The walk has no teetering.

CALL None

CONTEXT Probably done by female in front of male. Involved with courtship. May last several hours. *See* Courtship

Wing-Flutter

Male or Female   *Sp Su*

Bird holds wings partially extended and flutters tips. Bird may crouch down on the earth as if incubating.

CALL None

CONTEXT Done by two birds, probably a male and female during courtship. *See* Courtship

Back-Ruffle

Male or Female   *Sp Su*

Bird ruffles back feathers and runs in a horizontal or tilted-forward posture. Tail may be spread.

CALL None

CONTEXT Done in aggressive encounters between birds either on breeding ground or following breeding on feeding grounds. *See* Flock Behavior

Distraction Display
Male or Female   *Su*

The bird runs erratically, sometimes fluffing up into what looks like a little ball; wings may flutter and tail may be spread and dragging on the ground.

CALL Squeal-call

CONTEXT Done by either parent when the nest or young are in possible danger

Auditory Displays

The Song of the Spotted Sandpiper is a continuum of variations. At one end of the continuum is a series of rapid "weet" whistles, and at the other end the "weet" sounds are given more slowly and preceded by two or three introductory notes such as "peetaweet." All of the gradations between the two extremes are also given. Changes from one extreme to the other reflect changes in meaning. The two extremes are listed below, but expect to hear many of the gradations in between as well.

Aggressive-Song
Male or Female   *Sp Su*

weetweetweet or *weet weet weet*

A rapid series of short, ascending whistles. A long series tends to indicate extreme alarm; a series of two, three, or four whistles is more for aggression between birds.

CONTEXT Occurs during territory formation and moments of disturbance or alarm. Single whistles of "weet" may function as contact notes between the pair. *See* Territory, Flock Behavior

Courtship-Song

Male or Female *Sp Su*

A short whistle preceded by two or three short notes. This phrase is then repeated with intervals of a second or more in between.

CONTEXT Given in situations of courtship or other communication between the pair. Generally not given in situations of aggression

peetweet, peetweet or peetaweet peetaweet

Kerrwee-Call

Male or Female *Sp Su*

A low-pitched, rolling call that is usually given softly. Very different from the whistles of the Songs

CONTEXT Given by adults when near their young; seems to have the effect of bringing them together. *See* Breeding

Squeal-Call

Male or Female *Su*

A plaintive, screamlike call; often repeated several times in succession

CONTEXT Given by an adult during the Distraction Display. *See* Breeding

BEHAVIOR DESCRIPTIONS

Territory

Type: Mating, nesting
Size: Varies from a fraction of an acre to 3 or more acres
Main behavior: Chases, Aggressive-song
Duration: Spring to midsummer

The females are the first to arrive on the breeding ground and the ones that defend and compete over territories. Territorial defense takes the form of chases between females, often accompanied by the Aggressive-song. Males arrive later, and although they may chase one another, their interactions are more likely to be involved with establishing dominance within a female's territory. *See* Courtship.

The amount of territorial behavior in these birds depends a great deal on the density of the breeding area. On lake and coastal islands, breeding populations can be as dense as over a hundred pairs on only several acres. In other suitable breeding areas the birds are much more dispersed, with territories of over two acres for each pair. In these latter areas, territorial aggression occurs primarily at the beginning of the season, and boundaries become settled and rarely fought over after that. In more crowded areas, territorial borders may never be finally resolved, and aggressive encounters continue throughout the breeding season.

The birds tend to return to the same territories each year and often nest in the same spots. Territories mainly contain the nesting site, and feeding takes place at the edges of water in areas that are often shared by several birds.

Courtship

Main behavior: Strutting, chases, Wing-flutter

Generally, female Spotted Sandpipers arrive first and establish territories. Males arrive a few days later, returning to sites where they previously nested. In many cases, Spotted Sandpipers are polyandrous, with each female having several males as mates. Because of this the female tends to take the lead in territory formation and courtship.

When a male arrives, renewed aggression occurs between females and they may chase one another for long periods. Males may also chase other males to establish dominance within a given female's territory and the chance to pair with her. When chasing subsides, males and females may engage in displays.

The most commonly seen display in courtship is Strutting, where the female extends her neck, ruffles her throat feathers, and struts about in view of the male. This is often done along an open shoreline or on top of a fallen log by the shore. The birds may also do Wing-flutter (see Display Guide) or briefly chase one another. There is also a peculiar type of flight where the bird uses extremely rapid wingbeats and flies in a stalling manner with its body at a 45-degree angle. This is accompanied by one of the versions of the Song. In some cases, you can get a female to strut near you simply by imitating a version of the Song.

Pairing seems to occur rapidly in Spotted Sandpipers, almost within a few minutes of the start of courtship displays. After the displays, you may see paired birds make short runs into nesting areas, the male leading with tail down and the female following with tail up. These runs may be repeated in succession several times. The areas they run into are often where nesting will take place.

Once these short runs have occurred, the birds are firmly paired and remain close to one another, feeding together and giving single whistles of the Song to stay in contact. The closeness of the pair continues through the egg-laying phase. Once the female has finished laying the eggs, she may leave to court another male while her original mate stays to incubate the eggs and raise the young. Copulation occurs a day or two after pairing and nest-building, and egg-laying can be completed within five to six days after that.

Nest-Building

Placement: On the ground in grassy or weedy areas; nest site shaded by low vegetation
Size: Inside diameter 2½–3 inches; inside depth 1 inch
Materials: A shallow depression in the ground lined with grasses

Nest-building is not a conspicuous event with Spotted Sandpipers. The nest is just a shallow depression in the ground lined with a few grasses. It is completed within a day or two and egg-laying may start even before it is finished. It has not been clearly observed whether the male and/or the female does the building. The nest is always located so that vegetation shades it during the day, and although it is usually near water, it may be as far as a quarter-mile away.

If the birds are disturbed when the nest is being built, they often desert the site. Renesting in these cases is often at the opposite side of the territory.

Locating the Nest

WHERE TO LOOK In open areas along ponds, lakes, rivers, and seashores or on coastal islands

WHEN TO LOOK From midspring to midsummer

BEHAVIORAL CLUES TO NEST LOCATION:

1. Watch birds flushed out of nesting habit. They will probably circle back, land, and walk the final twenty to thirty feet to the nest.

2. Listen for the Aggressive-song given in response to your presence; this may indicate you are near the nest.

3. Only during the incubation phase can you locate the nest, for once hatched, the young leave the nest.

Breeding

Eggs: 4. Buff, with many brown spots
Incubation: 21 days, often by just male, but sometimes by male and female
Nestling phase: 2 or 3 days, or none
Fledgling phase: 3 weeks
Broods: 1

Egg-Laying and Incubation

Within a few days of pairing, the first egg is laid, sometimes even before the nest is complete. Eggs are usually laid one per day, although this may be interrupted by inclement weather, such as a storm or cold spell.

After laying the last egg in a given clutch, most females have a resurgence of sexual activity, calling and displaying to other males and fighting over the territory with other females. For some females, this leads to a pair bond with another male and a leaving of the first clutch. For others it means just a renewal of sexual and aggressive behavior for a few days; then they return to their original nest and participate in incubation and caring for the young.

Spotted Sandpipers have varying degrees of polyandry (more than one male per female). Some females have only a single male and in these cases the job of raising the young is often shared. Other females may lay clutches with as many as four or five different males. In these cases the males incubate the eggs and raise the young in all but the last clutch, where the female may participate.

During egg-laying, both birds may remain near the nest, but once incubation has started usually only one bird stays near. Incubation may start before the last egg is laid. As you approach a nest during incubation, the bird is likely to run a short distance from the nest and then fly off. When it feels there is no more danger, it will land near the nest and then run the rest of the way under cover. Some birds give a quiet version of Song as they return. Occasionally an undisturbed bird may give Song from the nest, seemingly in answer to another bird calling in the distance.

When disturbed at the nest by a potential predator, Spotted Sandpipers may perform a Distraction Display. This consists of fluttering along the ground with wings partly opened and tail spread and dragging on the ground. The Squeal-call is given during the display. This behavior is done in varying amounts by different individuals — some a lot, others not at all. You may see it as you approach a nest.

If a predator destroys the eggs in the nest, new clutches are usually started about five days later.

Nestling Phase

Young Spotted Sandpipers are able to leave the nest a few hours after hatching. The young remain in or near the nest until all the eggs have hatched, and in some cases this may take up to two days. Shells from hatched eggs are immediately carried from the nest.

Fledgling Phase

The young birds are watched over by either the male or the male and female for about three weeks. The family gradually moves away from the nest area and toward water or more open space. One of the parents may perch on a vantage point where it can see for a greater distance. It warns the young of danger by giving the Aggressive-song; this makes the fledglings freeze. When the parent gives the Kerrwee-call, the fledglings tend to come closer and gather near the parent. Sometimes at night a small, shallow depression is made in the earth in which the young remain while being brooded by the attentive parent. The parent, or parents, stay with the young until they are able to fly.

Plumage

DISTINGUISHING THE SEXES There is no way to be absolutely sure of the sexes from just appearance. Two partial clues are that the female tends to be larger than the male and more heavily spotted.

In terms of behavior, the male is often the only bird incubating eggs and caring for young, but this is certainly not always the case. The female tends to take the lead during courtship and territory defense.

DISTINGUISHING JUVENALS FROM ADULTS In mid- to late summer, the juvenals can be distinguished from adults by their clear, rather than spotted, breast. After the late-summer molt, young and adults cannot be distinguished, for both have unspotted breasts.

MOLTS Spotted Sandpipers undergo several stages of molting. In late summer to early fall, the birds molt their body feathers and the breast loses its spots and becomes clear white. Later in winter, probably after migration, the birds molt their tail and wing feathers. Then in March and April they again molt their body feathers and acquire the spotted breast so characteristic of the breeding season.

Seasonal Movement

Spotted Sandpipers are inconspicuous during migration since they rarely gather into large flocks and they seem to migrate by night. In the fall they migrate to South America and the islands in the Caribbean. In winter some birds are found in southern California and along the coast of southeastern states.

In spring they enter North America in late April and early May. Males and females arrive on the breeding ground a few at a time. Generally females arrive slightly earlier than males.

Flock Behavior

In late summer, groups of Spotted Sandpipers may gather in feeding areas. In some cases the birds seem to defend small feeding territories using the Aggressive-song and the Back-ruffle. In small areas, displaying can be intense and continue through much of the day.

On the wintering grounds, the birds have been observed to feed singly or in groups during the day and then each night gather into large communal roosts.

Mourning Dove / *Zenaida macroura*

MOURNING DOVES ARE EASILY ATTRACTED TO YOUR YARD BY A LITTLE cracked corn in an open area on the ground. This is ideal for the behavior-watcher since the birds feed in flocks and intersperse their feeding with exciting courtship and aggressive displays. These include Charging, where two birds run in tandem through the flock; Bow-coo, where one bird repeatedly bows its head and then gives the Long-coo; and Wing-raise, where a bird quickly raises one or both wings in a gesture of aggression.

Mourning Doves have only two basic calls, the Long-coo and the Short-coo. The former starts being given in early spring and continues throughout summer. Its sad, plaintive quality accounts for the bird's common name. The Long-coo is done most by unmated males in their effort to attract a female. During this period of courtship, they may also do their marvelous Flap-glide-flight, a flight display that has a pattern entirely different from the normal flight of the bird. The bird takes several deep up-and-down wing-beats, with the feathers hitting and making a clapping sound, then it glides with slightly down-turned wings. In this display it can easily be mistaken for a hawk — an American Kestrel in silhouette and a Sharp-shinned Hawk in flight pattern.

The Short-coo is just like the first three notes of the Long-coo. Be alert for this call, for it is usually given by a male from a nest or potential nest site. Hearing it indicates that a pair will be building a nest in the area. If this is the case, you have a good chance of seeing the male in the morning making frequent trips from the ground to the nest with twigs in his beak.

BEHAVIOR CALENDAR

	TERRITORY	COURTSHIP	NEST-BUILDING	BREEDING	PLUMAGE	SEASONAL MOVEMENT	FLOCK BEHAVIOR
JANUARY							▩
FEBRUARY							▩
MARCH	▩	▩	▩				▩
APRIL	▩	▩	▩	▩			
MAY	▩	▩	▩	▩			
JUNE	▩	▩	▩	▩			
JULY	▩	▩	▩	▩			
AUGUST	▩	▩		▩			
SEPTEMBER					▩		▩
OCTOBER					▩		▩
NOVEMBER					▩		▩
DECEMBER							▩

DISPLAY GUIDE

Visual Displays

Perch-Coo

Male   *Sp Su*

The bird sits erect, puffs out its throat, and bobs its tail.

CALL Long-coo

CONTEXT Done from perches, most frequently by unmated males to attract females. Done less frequently by mated males. *See* Courtship

Charging

Male or Female   *Sp Su F W*

Bird charges, or runs toward another bird, with head and tail horizontal. May end in a hop. Often followed by Bow-coo

CALL None

CONTEXT Given by males along with Bow-coo during courtship; given by either sex in aggressive encounters. Often seen at feeders. *See* Courtship

Bow-Coo

Male   *Sp Su*

Male bows down — sometimes repeatedly — until head nearly touches the ground, then lifts head and gives loud Long-coo.

CALL Long-coo

CONTEXT Done by males in front of females they are courting. May also be done by males to other males as part of territory defense. *See* Territory, Courtship

Flap-Glide-Flight

Male   *Sp Su*

Bird leaves perch and, with noisy flapping of wings as they touch under the body, rises up and then descends in a long, often spiraling glide with wings held slightly lower than the body. Makes the bird resemble a Sharp-shinned Hawk.

CALL None

CONTEXT Done by males — most often un-mated — during courtship to attract a female. Birds may do twelve or more flights in an hour and over a large area. Diminishes once pair bond is formed. *See* Territory, Courtship

Wing-Raise

Male or Female   *Sp Su F W*

Bird raises one or both wings and may even hit another bird with its wing. Sometimes a short wing-whistle sound occurs with a rapid raising and lowering of the wings.

CALL None

CONTEXT Usually occurs in aggressive encounters on the ground around feeders. Mourning Doves may also do this to other bird species and to small mammals such as squirrels.

Billing

Male or Female   *Sp Su*

The female puts her bill inside that of the male and they bob up and down several times.

CALL **None**
CONTEXT This occurs between members of a pair just before copulation. *See* Courtship

Auditory Displays

Long-Coo
Male, rarely Female   *Sp Su*

Five to seven cooing notes. The second note is stressed and higher pitched than the others.   *ooahoo oo oo oo*

CONTEXT Given throughout the breeding season, especially by unmated males, to attract a female. It is also used with the Bow-coo display in courtship and territory defense. *See* Territory, Courtship

Short-Coo
Male or Female   *Sp Su*

Three cooing notes, with the second note stressed and higher pitched than the others. Sounds just like the first three notes of the Long-coo.   *ooahoo*

CONTEXT Given most frequently by the male when calling the female to the nest site during nest-site selection or during nest-building. The female may give it to the male while she is on the nest. It is less frequent after the nest is completed. It can also be given during courtship or after territorial conflicts. *See* Nest-building

Mourning Doves make a whistling sound with their wings when flying, but they can also fly silently. The whistling sound may be a display.

BEHAVIOR DESCRIPTIONS

Territory

Type: Mating, nesting
Size: From 2- to 50-yard radius around the nest
Main behavior: Charging, Bow-coo, fighting
Duration: From the beginning of nest-building to the nestling phase

After pairing, a male will defend an area around the nest site. The area may be as large as one hundred yards in diameter during nest-building and egg-laying but then in later stages of breeding it diminishes to just a few yards around the nest. Male Doves respond to intruders with Bow-coo, Wing-raise, and Charging. Occasionally Mourning Doves are almost colonial, with several pairs building nests in the same tree.

Unmated males do not have a defined territory. Instead they tend to move about a large area, stopping at prominent perches from which they give their Perch-coo and try to attract a female. They do not defend the area or the perches, but occasionally, if other males come too close, they will chase them away, often doing Flap-glide-flight and sometimes hitting the other male.

The birds leave their territories to feed in flocks. When the birds are concentrated at a feeder there are many aggressive interactions. See Mourning Dove Feeder Behavior section.

Courtship

Main behavior: Perch-coo, Bow-coo, Charging, Flap-glide-flight, three-bird chases, copulation
Duration: From pairing through egg-laying

The beginning of Mourning Dove courtship marks the start of what is probably the most conspicuous and familiar of Mourning Dove behavior: Perch-cooing. This is given primarily by unmated males to attract a female. Interspersed with Perch-cooing, males will do Flap-glide-flight, where they leave their perch with a loud clapping of wings and rise up to one hundred feet or more, then spiral down with wings held slightly below the body, looking more like the silhouette of an American Kestrel than a Mourning Dove. Once a bird is paired, these displays are less frequently given.

Sometimes during this period you may see chases involving three birds, usually a female and two males. These three-bird chases occur most frequently when a mated pair flies by an unmated male and he flies up after them.

During courtship you will also see males approaching females on the ground and doing Charging followed by Bow-coo, or landing near a female on a perch and doing just the Bow-coo. The female may move a short distance, in which case the male usually follows her and repeats his displays, or she may fly away with the male in pursuit. If she stays near the male, the two are likely to copulate.

Before copulation, the female may preen and then both birds may preen each other, with the female possibly crouching down and vibrating her wings. Then Billing usually occurs, with the female putting her beak into the male's and the two bobbing their heads together. He will then step on top of her and mate. Following copulation, there may be self- and/or mutual preening. Copulation usually occurs in the male's territory.

Nest-Building

*Placement: In a vertical fork or horizontal branch of a tree, 3–30 feet
above the ground, or, rarely, on the ground
Size: Outside diameter 8–12 inches
Materials: Twigs, grass, weeds, pine needles*

Selection of the nest site is begun by the male. He flies to a potential spot, such as a horizontal limb, and gives the Short-coo. He may repeat this on several succeeding days until the female responds and flies up to him. Both birds may then give softer Short-coos and mutually preen one another. The male may constantly flip his wings when he gives Short-coo, and when the female joins him, she may get on the nest site and flip her wings as well.

The male brings the nest material up to the female, one piece at a time. He collects it on the ground fairly near the nest site and may pick up and discard several pieces before he selects one. When he reaches the female, he may stand next to her and give her the piece or he may stand on her back while he transfers the piece to her over her shoulder. Sometimes the male may peck the female under the chin, give a soft Short-coo, and then change places with her on the nest. While on the nest, he may rearrange some of the nest material. Nest-building usually takes place for several hours each morning until the nest is completed and can take from one to six days to complete.

The nest is a loosely made, flat platform that often does not stand up well in storms. Sometimes Mourning Doves will reuse their old nests or those of other doves or species, adding a little material of their own.

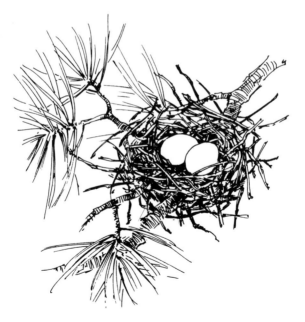

Locating the Nest

WHERE TO LOOK In trees along open areas

WHEN TO LOOK From March to September

BEHAVIORAL CLUES TO NEST LOCATION:

    1. Listen for the nest call.

    2. Watch for male Dove walking around the ground picking up pieces of grass or twigs, and follow him to the nest site.

Breeding

Eggs: Average 2. White
Incubation: 14–15 days, by male and female
Nestling phase: 12–13 days
Fledgling phase: 1 week or more
Broods: 1–2

Egg-Laying and Incubation

Incubation starts just before or after the laying of the last egg. Male and female Mourning Doves share in incubation and the birds have an amazing schedule — the male incubates the eggs without once leaving the nest from morning until evening, and the female does the same from evening until morning. The changeover takes place between 8:30 and 10:30 in the morning and between 4:30 and 5:30 in the evening.

When a Mourning Dove is frightened off its nest, it may just fly to another tree, or it may do a distraction display, in which it acts as though it were injured. It will fall to the ground and hop and flutter about. This behavior can be given by males and females and is more likely to occur in the more advanced part of the nesting cycle when the eggs have hatched and there are young in the nest.

Nestling Phase

The young may be slightly different sizes because they hatch one or two days apart. Parents feed the young "pigeon milk," nutritious whitish liquid the parents regurgitate. The young put their bills inside the parent's and the parent pumps the food up. Toward the end of the nestling phase, an increasing percentage of the food is regurgitated seeds and insects. The parents brood the young almost constantly until they are about ten days old. The young are capable of flying from the nest at this age and may do so if disturbed, but will leave voluntarily at twelve or thirteen days. The Mourning Dove is unusual in that it does not remove the feces of the young from the nest. Feedings of the young are spaced far apart, for the adults spend a great deal of time gathering food in their crops and then regurgitate it all at once to the young in the nest.

Fledgling Phase

The young may remain in the nest tree for up to six days, and they may roost in the nest for the first two or three nights of the fledgling phase. Within a week or more they are on their own and feed in flocks of other juvenals and adults.

Plumage

DISTINGUISHING THE SEXES The differences between the sexes are subtle. The male has a rose-tinted breast and a grayish top to its head, while the female is more dull brown all over her chest and head. In terms of behavior, the male is the only one that does Perch-coo, Bow-coo, and Flap-glide-flight displays and is the one that carries the twigs to the female during nest-building.

DISTINGUISHING JUVENAL FROM ADULT Juvenals lack the black spot behind the eye that is present in the adults; they have shorter tails, and their wing and breast feathers are edged with light buff.

MOLTS Adults have one complete molt per year and it occurs from September to November.

Flock Behavior

During winter most Mourning Doves feed and roost together in flocks containing twenty to fifty birds or more. These flocks drift about a given area as food sources change. Flocks in the northern states seem to have a higher percentage of males. There is also some evidence suggesting that these flocks may remain fairly stable in membership through winter and even have a fixed social hierarchy called "peck dominance," in which certain birds are generally dominant over others.

Feeder Behavior

Mourning Doves are marvelous birds to watch at your feeder because practically all of their courtship behavior can be observed there. Aggressive interactions over food are common as well. See Display Guide and sections on Courtship, Territory, Seasonal Movement, and Flock Behavior.

MOST COMMON DISPLAYS Look for birds at ground feeders doing Charging and Bow-coo displays in aggressive encounters and as part of courtship. They will also do Wing-raise to other Mourning Doves and other bird species, as well as to squirrels. Unmated males will Perch-coo from up in trees as they try to attract females. They may even try to land on the back of females and mate.

OTHER BEHAVIOR If you hear the Short-coo, look for the nest. You may also see mating, three-bird chases, and Flap-glide-flight.

Belted Kingfisher / *Megacyrle alcyon*

KINGFISHERS ARE USUALLY HEARD BEFORE THEY ARE SEEN, FOR THEIR Rattle-call travels far and is easily recognized. A common experience is to be by a stream or river and hear a Kingfisher give the Rattle-call as it swoops overhead and flies upstream. You lose sight of it until you come closer, when it again calls and flies farther. The bird will continue to do this until it reaches the end of its territory along the stream, then it will circle back, often without your knowing. In spring and summer, pairs of Kingfishers defend territories, which contain both a nest site and fishing area, although the two may not be adjacent. When breeding is over, the pair separate and each defends a smaller feeding territory through fall and winter.

The nest of the Kingfisher is truly remarkable. It is excavated in the ground and consists of a long tunnel with a large space at the end. The nest is not as hard to find as one might expect. You don't look for the nest at first, but rather for a steep cutaway bank clear of vegetation. The bank may be beside water, at the edge of a road, or along an old gravel pit. About a foot or two from the top, look for a tunnel three to four inches in diameter. If you find one, there is a good chance it is a Kingfisher nest. Look at the bottom edge of the entrance: if there are two slight grooves there, you can be sure to have found a nest, since these are the tracks worn by the birds' feet as they enter and leave. If there are no spider webs in the entrance and a little fresh earth below it, then the nest is probably active. (*See* Nest-building.)

BEHAVIOR CALENDAR

	TERRITORY	COURTSHIP	NEST-BUILDING	BREEDING	PLUMAGE	SEASONAL MOVEMENT	FLOCK BEHAVIOR
JANUARY	▓						
FEBRUARY	▓						
MARCH	▓	▓				▓	
APRIL	▓	▓	▓	▓		▓	
MAY	▓	▓	▓	▓			
JUNE	▓	▓	▓	▓			
JULY	▓			▓			
AUGUST	▓			▓	▓	▓	
SEPTEMBER	▓				▓	▓	
OCTOBER	▓				▓		
NOVEMBER	▓						
DECEMBER	▓						

DISPLAY GUIDE

Visual Displays

Crest-Raise

Male or Female   *Sp Su F W*

Bird raises the feathers on its crest

CALL Rattle-call, or none

CONTEXT Done in moments of excitement or danger

Head/Tail-Bob

Male or Female   *Sp Su F W*

Bird bobs head and/or tail

CALL None, or Rattle-call

CONTEXT Given in moments of aggression toward other Kingfishers

Auditory Displays

Rattle-Call

Male or Female   *Sp Su F W*

A fast series of harsh sounds that form a   *k'k'k'k'k'k*
continuous rattle-like call. May be a short
volley or a long continuous rattle

CONTEXT Probably the most familiar call of the Kingfisher and given in a variety of circumstances. It is usually loud when given during territorial encounters or moments of alarm, but also may be soft and conversational when given between mates. This is the only common call of the Belted Kingfisher. Various other calls have been reported in the literature, but they are not described clearly enough to include them here. It may be that the Rattle-call is a graded communication system with long, loud volleys having one meaning and short, quiet volleys another meaning. For an example of this, see the Song of the Spotted Sandpiper.

BEHAVIOR DESCRIPTIONS

Territory

Kingfishers defend a breeding territory in spring and summer and a nonbreeding territory in fall and winter.

Breeding Territory

Type: Mating, nesting, feeding
Size: On small streams; average is about 1000 yards of stream length
Main behavior: Rattle-call, chases, Head/tail-bob
Duration of defense: From male arrival on breeding ground until the end of fledgling phase

When males first arrive on the breeding ground in early spring, they begin to defend a nest site. When the female arrives, she seems to be attracted to the nest site and then pairs with the male. The two then defend the nest site and a fishing area. The main displays used in defense are the Rattle-call and the Head/tail-bob. Direct attacks and fierce chases may also be seen.

Nest sites and fishing sites are the two most important areas for Kingfishers, but the two are not always in the same place. Streams and lakes with good fishing may have no suitable banks in which the birds can nest. In such cases the birds may travel a mile or more away from their fishing site to find a nest site. Thus you may see aggressive conflicts between Kingfishers on lakes where there are no nesting areas, or between birds in woods or clearings with no water nearby.

Nonbreeding Territory

Type: Feeding
Size: On small streams; average is 500 yards of stream length
Main behavior: Rattle-call, chases, Head/tail-bob
Duration: From shortly after the fledgling phase until the start of the next breeding season

One of the most common times to contact Kingfishers is when you are boating on a river or walking up a stream. When you intrude on a bird's territory, you will immediately hear the Rattle-call and possibly see the bird fly on ahead of you. It will repeat this behavior until it reaches the limit of its territory. It will then circle back behind you. This is one way you can get an estimate of Kingfisher territory size.

A few weeks after the fledgling stage ends, all Kingfishers — young and adults, males and females — defend individual feeding territories. These are usually about half the size of breeding territories. They tend to be less permanent, for if the water freezes over or flooding occurs, the birds will abandon their territories and move to where they can more easily feed. If the freeze thaws or the flood subsides, the territories may be reoccupied. Displays used in defending these territories are the same as those used during the breeding season.

Kingfishers are exciting to watch as they feed, for they either sit on perches or hover in the air and then dive into the water to catch fish.

Courtship

Main behavior: Birds of a pair remaining closely associated
Duration: From arrival of female until end of breeding

Males seem to arrive first on the breeding ground and often remain near a nest site. Females arrive slightly later. Pairing seems to take place with very few displays. Once paired, the two tend to stay together and share in activities. A curious behavior of Kingfishers at this time takes place high in the air. Several birds fly up together, rising several hundred feet, and circle about and chase each other and give the Rattle-call, as well as other sounds. The function of these flights is not known.

Once breeding is over, the pair separate and keep to their own territories until the next spring.

Nest-Building

Placement: In the ground with a horizontal entrance starting 1–3 feet below the top of a cutaway bank
Size: Entrance hole 3–4 inches in diameter
Materials: Nest excavated in earth; no additional materials

Belted Kingfishers' nests are excavated in the ground and consist of a long tunnel leading to a rounded chamber where the eggs are laid and the young raised.

The birds nest in steep banks of bare ground. They prefer to nest in tall banks and usually start their tunnel about a foot or a foot and a half below the top of the bank where topsoil gives way to sand. They may nest along streams, shore, ocean banks, or in man-made road banks or gravel pits. Sandy, clay soil is preferred, and the birds may start a tunnel and then abandon it for better soil. Probe holes may be seen near a nest tunnel; these are where the bird tested for suitable soil. Sites are usually free of vegetation, and there is almost always a dead limb within one hundred feet on which the birds can perch and see the nest. The tunnel may be as narrow as three inches at the entrance and may narrow further to two inches. Tunnel length averages three to six feet but may be ten to fifteen feet in rare cases. It can be straight, or curved if the birds encountered some resistance, such as a rock or root, and it usually slopes up to the chamber. A distinctive feature of the tunnel and its entrance is that there are usually two slight grooves on the lower edge. These are caused by the feet of the birds as they walk in and out of the tunnel, and they are a good way to help you distinguish Kingfisher nests from other holes in the ground.

The nest cavity at the end of the tunnel is like a flattened sphere with loose earth on the floor. It is nine to twelve inches in diameter and about six to eight inches high.

Most excavation is done with the bill. The birds take turns excavating and each time one enters the tunnel it kicks back with its feet, scraping out earth loosened by the other bird's excavation. The scraping can be so forceful that the earth streams out of the hole like a fountain. A foot or more of the tunnel can be dug in a day, and it takes from a few days to a week or two to complete the nest. When not digging, the birds rest on a perch near the entrance to the hole. This perch may even have excavated earth along it from the birds' feet. In some cases the birds' bills may be seriously worn down at the tip from excavation.

Nest sites may or may not be near water. *See* Breeding Territory

Breeding

Eggs: 5–7, usually 6. White
Incubation: 22–26 days
Nestling phase: 18–28 days
Fledgling phase: 1–2 weeks
Broods: 1

Egg-Laying and Incubation
Both male and female have well-developed brood patches and both incubate the eggs. In some cases the female has been known to

incubate the eggs during the night while the male roosts nearby. When coming to the nest, the birds first land on a perch nearby and give the Rattle-call. From there they fly directly into the nest, often so rapidly that you may not be able to see whether the bird is male or female. The birds also tend to give the Rattle-call as they leave the nest.

Nestling Phase

For the first few days of the nestling phase, the female may brood the young while the male brings the majority of food. The parents collect food for the young from as early as 4:00 A.M. to as late as 11:00 P.M. The least amount of feeding occurs in midafternoon, especially on hot days. Feedings may occur as often as every twenty minutes, and trips in and out of the nest may be accomplished in a minute or less. In many instances the male seems to do twice as much feeding of the young as the female does.

The nestlings have an interesting pattern of feather development. They are born without any feathers, but within a week, all of their feathers have appeared in their sheaths and remain that way, unopened, for the next two weeks or slightly less. In this stage they look like porcupines. On their seventeenth or eighteenth day after hatching, all of their feathers burst from their sheaths within twenty-four hours.

The nestlings do not have fecal sacs, but rather eject liquid feces against the walls of the nest chamber. After defecating, they indiscriminately peck earth from the sides of the cavity walls. This may function to bury previously dried feces. The pecking habit tends to make the nest cavity get shallower as the floor builds up with loose earth. The young birds have a special blunt, hardened tip to their bill for the first half of their nestling life. This may be to protect their still-soft bills from injury as they peck at the nest-cavity walls. The tip is shed when the feather sheaths break and the bill hardens.

The young can fly when they leave the nest.

Fledgling Phase

During the first few days of this phase, the young perch in protected places near the parents. The whole family tends to stay within one hundred yards of each other, and the parents give the Rattle-call a great deal as they catch fish and feed them to the young. Some observers believe the young are taught how to fish by the parents; others believe that they can learn on their own. In any case, the young are able to catch fish after a week or two of leaving the nest.

Birds often use the same perches again and again, and on the ground beneath these spots you are likely to see the whitewash from their droppings and small pellets of bones that the birds cast from their mouth.

Plumage

DISTINGUISHING THE SEXES The adults are easily distinguished through plumage, for the female has a rusty band of feathers across her breast while the male's breast is all white.

DISTINGUISHING JUVENALS FROM ADULTS They are similar to the adults except that their upper breast band is brownish instead of blue.

MOLTS Adults undergo one complete molt per year, between August and October.

Seasonal Movement

Many Belted Kingfishers remain in the northern states through winter, especially along the East and West coasts. They stay in areas where there is open water and they can continue to catch fish. When these areas freeze they move as far as they have to, to find open water.

Other Kingfishers migrate south, some as far as Central America and the northern portions of South America. This occurs in September through November. Wherever they winter, the birds defend small feeding territories. *See* Territory.

Birds that have migrated return north in March and April.

Downy Woodpecker / *Picoides pubescens*

THE DOWNY WOODPECKER IS A VERY ENDEARING BIRD, FOR IT WILL become a regular visitor to your feeder if you provide a little suet in a string bag. A nice feature of Downies is that you can easily distinguish not only the sexes — the male having a red head patch and the female none — but also individual birds. The patterns of black and white on the back of their head vary a great deal, and if you make a rough sketch of this pattern from your birds, you will know how many different males or females are around your house.

In many cases, male and female Downies lead somewhat separate lives in fall and early winter. A pair may remain on the same territory but they will not feed together; and if they get too close, the male will be aggressive to the female. Then in late winter, a sign that their behavior is about to change is the Drumming that the birds do on selected resonant trees in their territory. Male and female have separate Drumming posts. Drumming functions both to advertise territory to other woodpeckers and to keep the pair in closer touch with each other.

Over the next two to three months the pair increasingly synchronize their activities. A crucial point in their lives is when they choose a tree in which to excavate their nest hole. If the pair cannot agree on a site, it means they may not successfully breed; but if they can agree, the nest becomes the center of all the rest of their activities until the young fledge.

BEHAVIOR CALENDAR

	TERRITORY	COURTSHIP	NEST-BUILDING	BREEDING	PLUMAGE	SEASONAL MOVEMENT	FLOCK BEHAVIOR
JANUARY	■						
FEBRUARY	■	■					
MARCH	■	■				■	
APRIL	■	■	■	■		■	
MAY	■		■	■			
JUNE	■		■	■			
JULY	■			■			
AUGUST	■				■		
SEPTEMBER	■				■	■	
OCTOBER	■						
NOVEMBER	■						
DECEMBER	■						

DISPLAY GUIDE

Visual Displays

Bill-Waving

Male or Female   W Sp

The bird repeatedly waves its bill from left to right. Wings may be flicked and the tail may be spread and flicked from side to side. Sometimes the wings are fully raised and the bill gaped.

CALL Queek-queek-call

CONTEXT Usually given between two birds of the same sex as both birds face each other on a tree limb. May be alternated with periods of Still-pose. *See* Territory, Courtship

Crest-Raise

Male or Female   Sp Su F W

The feathers at the top and back of the head are raised. In the males this makes their red head patch more evident.

CALL None

CONTEXT Given in times of excitement; may accompany other displays

Still-Pose

Male or Female   W Sp Su

After interacting, two birds suddenly stop all movement and remain absolutely still for one to twenty minutes.

CALL None

CONTEXT Occurs primarily during sexual or territorial encounters. *See* Territory

V-Wing

Male or Female   W Sp Su

Wings are raised high above the back and tail is spread. Display may be for only a split second or held for several seconds. Bird may swing beneath a branch and do display upside down.

CALL None

CONTEXT Given in conflicts with other birds; an extreme threat, often preceding direct attack. *See* Territory, Nest-building

Fluttering-Flight

Male or Female   W Sp

The bird flies slowly with rapid fluttering wingbeats. Entirely different from the normal swooping flight.

CALL Queek-queek-call

CONTEXT Given in courtship; often near a nest, and sometimes just before copulation. Seen during nest-building and egg-laying and again near the end of the nestling phase. *See* Courtship

Auditory Displays

Teak-Call

Male or Female   Sp Su F W

teak.teak. teak, teak. A single loud note, sometimes repeated at irregular intervals

CONTEXT Generally given as a contact note between members of a pair

Whinny-Call

Male or Female   Sp Su F

A one- or two-second burst of staccato notes

that descend in pitch near the end. Sounds like the whinny of a miniature horse.

CONTEXT Used as a long-distance location call between members of a pair and as an aggressive call during territorial conflicts and courtship. Also heard from fledglings. *See* Territory, Courtship, Breeding

Queek-Queek-Call

Male or Female W Sp

Three to five short notes given in series. Fairly loud and with a definite "excited" sound

queekqueekqueekqueek

CONTEXT Given during Bill-waving, Fluttering-flight, and other behavior associated with courtship. *See* Courtship

Drumming

Male or Female W Sp

One- or two-second bursts of loud and rapid pecking on resonant surfaces. May be repeated frequently and regularly, and may be answered by another Downy Woodpecker.

CONTEXT Given from specific posts within the territory and used to announce territory, attract a new mate, or call a mate to a given spot. *See* Territory, Courtship, Nest-building

Fledgling-Calls

Male or Female Sp Su

The last few days in the nest, the young give constant high-pitched calls from the nest entrance. Once out of the nest, they seem to develop a version of the Whinny-call that is lighter and higher than that of the adults. They also occasionally use a lighter version of the Teak-call.

CONTEXT These occur especially when the parents are near and the young are looking for food from them. *See* Breeding

BEHAVIOR DESCRIPTIONS

Territory

Type: Nesting, mating
Size: ¼ acre
Main behavior: Drumming, chases, and many displays
Duration: From late winter through breeding

The first sign of Downy territorial behavior is Drumming: loud, rapid bursts of pecking on resonant surfaces. This starts in late winter and continues until the end of spring. Both members of a pair Drum and each tends to have its own favorite Drumming posts within their range. Downies Drum repeatedly from a given post and then may move on to another and start again. It is common to hear other Downies Drum in response from their own ranges, and this creates a duet or, in some cases, trio, with the birds continually answering each other's bouts.

Through Drumming, pairs gradually establish the extent of their range, which may vary from five to thirty-five acres. Ranges of neighboring Downies may overlap, and thus no pair attempts to defend the range strictly. When aggressive interactions occur on the range, they are often in the vicinity of Drumming posts or possible nest sites. They usually involve just two birds, of the same sex, chasing after each other and doing a variety of displays. The displays include Bill-waving, Frozen-pose, V-wing, and Queek-queek-call. Chases involve the two birds hitching around the sides of trees, one bird diving at another, and last-second evasive action by the bird being dived at. These may be short or continue for an hour or more. The range usually contains the winter roost holes for the pair and is where feeding and courtship occur.

In spring, Downy pairs establish a real territory, which they defend against all other Downies. Territory is within the range, and signs of its early formation are that the pair begin to frequent one spot within the range. This spot will have prospective nest trees and will become a center of interest for the birds. They will begin to defend it strictly, and finally will excavate a nest in it. The territory is small, usually about forty to one hundred feet in diameter. Once egg-laying starts, the defense of it becomes a high priority, and the birds spend less time patrolling the range.

Ranges and territories tend to be used by the same birds year after year. In late winter, resident birds reestablish their ranges and territories gradually over a period of several months. Migrant Downies arrive later, and, as a result, their territorial behavior is condensed in time and seemingly more intense.

Aggressive interactions between Downies in winter usually stem from competition for roosting holes or prime feeding areas. Some Downies may drift off their ranges in winter to areas where there is more food; others may migrate, but the majority are residents all year.

Courtship

Main behavior: Drumming, Whinny-call, chases
Duration: Late winter to late spring

For the majority of the year, midsummer to late winter, the male and female of a Downy pair lead fairly separate lives. If there is adequate food, resident pairs may remain on their territories; if there is not, one or both members may leave. In competition for food, the male is more dominant at this time of year, diving at the female and displacing her from perches.

The first sign of courtship in late winter is the sound of the Whinny-call or Drumming. Through these two displays, the members of a pair seem to answer each other and keep more in touch with each other's movements. After several days of long-distance contact, Drumming and the Whinny-call tend to make the pair come closer and the birds start to do more of their activities together.

An important part in the courtship of Downies is the establishment of a nesting tree. During the time that the birds start to remain closer together, they will move about and explore various trees that might make suitable nest sites. If a good tree is found and the two agree on it, that is, both excavate at the same spot, then the pair will form a strong bond. If the pair do not agree, or no tree is found, the pair are more likely to separate. The nest tree becomes a center of interest for the birds, and much of their most active behavior can be seen around it. Fluttering-flight is seen in this area particularly, often with the bird landing on the nest tree.

Two other aspects of Downy courtship are triangle encounters and copulation. Triangle encounters involve a lone bird trying to get a mate from a mated pair and being attacked by the same-sex bird of the mated pair. Bill-waving and direct attacks are the main aggressive displays, the intruding bird doing mostly evasive actions. The bird that is being fought over generally remains in the area of the fight and may give the Queek-queek-call in an increasingly excited fashion. Triangle encounters may continue for an hour or more and may be repeated over several days.

Copulations start in May and usually occur within fifteen yards of the nest hole. The female assumes an unusual posture for woodpeckers — perching across a branch, with head up and tail straight out. The male flies to the female, sometimes with Fluttering-flight, hovers briefly behind her, and then lands on her back. As he moves off to the left side of her, he bends his tail down and mates. The two remain in this position for several seconds and then the male gets off.

Nest-Building

*Placement: Nests are excavated in dead trees, often near the top of a bro-
ken stub 5–40 feet high.*
*Size: Nest hole entrance 1¼ inch in diameter; inside tree, hole goes down
8–10 inches.*
*Materials: There is no lining, just a few wood chips in the bottom of the
hole.*

During courtship, both male and female start to explore trees
that may be suitable for a nest hole. Nest holes are excavated in
dead wood, often in broken stubs of trees. Each bird may start bits
of excavation in various trees at first, but the pair's ability to choose
a final location and both work on it is essential to successful
breeding. Final nest-site selection seems to be guided by the
suitability of the stub, the dominance of each member of the pair,
and how these particular birds have used the area in previous
seasons. In any case, just because you see Downies excavating,
don't assume that will be the final nest site.

Excavation may continue for a week or two, with the male doing
the majority of the work. Fresh chips beneath a tree hole indicate a
currently excavated nest. The tapping involved in excavation is
fairly loud and consists of irregular pecking sounds. Once the hole
is deep enough, the bird excavates from inside,and all you may
notice are the pecking sounds, and bits of sawdust periodically
being tossed out the entrance. Excavating most often takes place in
the morning.

During the excavation period you will hear Drumming and
Whinny-calls from the area of the nest and see Fluttering-flight as
the birds leave or approach the nest. During the later stages of
excavation, you have a good chance to see copulation on a nearby
perch.

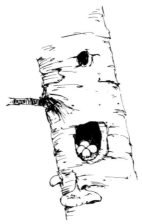

Nest hole above with portion cut away to show eggs

Locating the Nest

WHERE TO LOOK In forests where trees are old enough to have large dead portions

WHEN TO LOOK In spring

BEHAVIORAL CLUES TO NEST LOCATION:

1. Watch for close interactions between the pair, for these usually occur near the nest.

2. Listen for continual, regular, loud tapping, which is excavation rather than Drumming or the quieter, more irregular tapping of food searching.

Breeding

Eggs: 4–5. White
Incubation: 12 days
Nestling phase: 20–22 days
Fledgling phase: Up to 3 weeks
Broods: 1, occasionally 2 in south

Egg-Laying and Incubation

During egg-laying, the pair keep a close watch over the nest. Egg-laying may take four to six days and the eggs are probably not incubated until near the end of this period. During egg-laying, Downies spend about 40 percent of the time near or in the nest. When in the nest, but not incubating, the bird remains in the entrance, looking out.

When full incubation begins, there is always one bird regularly at the nest, and the birds generally relieve each other in a fixed fashion. The approaching bird lands silently at the side of the nest and sometimes taps somewhere about the side of the cavity, at which point the bird inside sticks its head out and flies off. The other bird then goes in. Usually the birds arrive and leave from the nest site with Fluttering-flight. Occasionally the incubating bird leaves briefly to preen and then goes back in, or it may leave altogether before the other arrives, in which case the other tends to show up in a minute or two. Each bird averages thirty to sixty minutes on the nest before the other bird relieves it. Males stay on the nest through the night.

Copulation is frequent during egg-laying and continues slightly into the incubation period.

Nestling Phase

There is a marked change in the behavior of the adults when the young hatch. Periods on the nest are shorter and more irregular than during incubation. The parents start to bring food to the nest and fecal sacs are carried away (although on occasion they are eaten). The eggs hatch over one or two days, and by the second day the parent birds may be making frequent trips, as often as every five to ten minutes. The young are fed directly, and usually only one bird is fed on each trip. The young are brooded for the first two weeks in the nest, and by the end of that period for only a small portion of the day. The brooding during the day is shared, but the male continues to spend the night on the nest.

The behavior of the feeding parent can help you estimate the age of the nestlings. The parent reaches all the way inside the nest for the first nine days to feed the young. On the tenth through twelfth days, it just reaches into the top of the nest. On the remaining days it feeds the young at the entrance.

The calls of the young are faint until the birds are reaching their heads out of the nest hole; then they can be heard fifty to one hundred yards away. After the birds leave the nest, this call changes into the Whinny-call.

Fledgling Phase

During the last day of the nestling phase, the parents all but stop feeding the young, and the young spend their time squeezing farther and farther out of the nest. When they leave, they are able to take flight immediately. During the fledgling and late nestling phase, the parents start to Drum and give the Whinny-call. This is believed to be a renewal of sexual behavior. It wanes once the young have emerged.

For at least the first week, the young and parents remain in the area of the nest. While the young are still dependent, they give location calls for the parent: loud and often repeated "tchicks," and a version of the Whinny-call. Upon receiving food, the young may raise or flick their wings and wave their beak from side to side. They follow the parents around and seem even aggressive at times as they try to get food. Sometimes the parents do aggressive displays toward them, such as the V-wing or Crest-raise. It may be these aggressive interactions that eventually cause the young to disperse.

Plumage

DISTINGUISHING THE SEXES Males at all stages can be told from females by the presence of the red patch on the back of their head. The variability of the back-of-the-head patterns on both sexes can often enable you to distinguish between individuals of the same sex.

DISTINGUISHING JUVENALS FROM ADULTS Fledglings in general can be told from adults by the clearly new, white feathers on their breast. Adults have gone in and out of the nest hole hundreds of times by this stage and look very worn, with bits of black showing through their white breast feathers. The fledgling male has some red on the top of the head rather than on the back of the head.

MOLTS The birds undergo one complete molt per year, from mid-August to mid-September.

Seasonal Movement

Downies may or may not migrate in any given year. What determines this is not known but may have to do with availability of food. In areas where there is plenty of food, the birds are often residents all year. Where there is not enough food, the birds may drift to new areas or actually migrate. Females tend to migrate more than males. Birds that have migrated return in March and April.

Feeder Behavior

Offer suet at your feeder and Downies will become regular visitors. You may get more than one pair, for the birds' winter ranges often overlap. In late winter you may notice that the male and female are more closely associated; this is an indication that courtship has begun. If you continue to offer suet through summer, the adults may bring their young to the feeder.

Generally, males are dominant over females at the feeder and will often supplant them. See the section on Plumage to learn how to recognize individual Downies. *See* Display Guide, Courtship, and Territory.

MOST COMMON DISPLAYS Supplanting (see chapter on "Bird Feeders and Behavior-Watching"), Crest-raise, Teak-call, Whinny-call, Queek-queek-call

OTHER DISPLAYS If you have good, resonant dead limbs on some of the trees near your house, a Downy may select one for a Drumming post (hopefully he'll pass up your drainpipe). Most of the other Visual Displays will take place away from the feeder during territorial and courtship encounters.

Eastern Phoebe / *Sayornis phoebe*

THE EASTERN PHOEBE IS ONE OF THE EARLIEST MIGRANTS IN SPRING, often arriving while there are still patches of snow on the ground or before the last cold spell. Soon after the males arrive, they begin to sing and give the Chirp-call as they patrol their territories. This is the bird's most conspicuous period and the best time to locate territorial males because not many other birds are singing and there are very few leaves on trees to hide the bird's activities.

Once the female has arrived and paired with the male, the birds are harder to find, since the male stops most of his singing during the day and the two move about quietly, using just the Chirp-call to keep in contact.

The Phoebe is loved by many for its habit of building its mud nest nearby on buildings, such as on barns or the eaves of houses. Once a pair have found a good spot, they return year after year and may even build a new nest on top of the old one. Nests on a porch can be both a blessing and a nuisance: the birds are close and you can watch all of their behavior, but their droppings also fall on the floor beneath. Farther away from humans, Phoebes favor bridges or culverts for their nests.

Phoebes often have a second brood in early summer and this is marked by renewed Song from the male and remodeling of the first nest by the female.

BEHAVIOR CALENDAR

	TERRITORY	COURTSHIP	NEST-BUILDING	BREEDING	PLUMAGE	SEASONAL MOVEMENT	FLOCK BEHAVIOR
JANUARY							
FEBRUARY							
MARCH	▓	▓				▓	
APRIL	▓	▓	▓	▓			
MAY	▓	▓	▓	▓			
JUNE	▓			▓			
JULY				▓			
AUGUST					▓		
SEPTEMBER					▓	▓	
OCTOBER						▓	
NOVEMBER							
DECEMBER							

DISPLAY GUIDE

Visual Displays

Raised-Crown

Male or Female   *Sp Su F W*

The bird raises the feathers on its crown in varying degrees.

CALL Chirp-call

CONTEXT Given when there is danger near the nest or in moments of aggressive excitement

Wing-Flutter

Male or Female   *Sp Su*

The bird's wings are lifted high over its back and rapidly beat in a shallow arc. Done while either perched or flying

CALL None or Chatter-call when done by a male; none when done by female

CONTEXT Given by the male or female silently prior to copulation, and also given by the male when he is "showing" the female a nest site

Flight-Display

Male   *Sp*

The bird flies out into an open area with rapid wingbeats and erratic flight path. Flight may rise high in the air.

CALL Any of the bird's calls

CONTEXT Given in early spring and associated with territory formation. *See* Territory

Auditory Displays

Song

Male or Female   *Sp Su F*

feebee. feebee.   Generally a two-part sound: a high-pitched, ascending note followed by a short rasping note. It sounds much like a hoarse rendition of its name.

CONTEXT Given primarily by males from arrival on the breeding ground until their nest has been started. It may be heard from unmated males at any time of day; mated males generally give it only in a regular predawn session. *See* Territory, Courtship

Chirp-Call

Male or Female   *Sp Su F W*

A short, single, moderately harsh "chip"

CONTEXT Given by members of a pair when there is any disturbance near the nest, often combined with Crest-raise. Given by the male either during patrolling or during the morning rendezvous, often after landing from short flights. Some consider the calls used in these latter instances to be a separate display, but most observers will have trouble distinguishing them. *See* Territory, Courtship

T'keet-Call

Male or Female   *Sp Su*

t'keet t'keet   A short, harsh call, distinguished from the Chirp-call by having two brief syllables instead of one

CONTEXT Usually given during aggressive encounters between mates, or as a female responds aggressively to a male's nearness or his copulation attempts. Sometimes given during chases between mated birds

Chatter-Call

Male   *Sp*

A rapid series of harsh chips that sounds like   *ch'ch'ch'ch'ch*
a chatter. The Phoebe's only call with a rapid
series of sounds

CONTEXT Given by males, usually as they do Wing-fluttering display. This is used primarily in the presence of a mate, and always during nest-site showing. *See* Nest-building

BEHAVIOR DESCRIPTIONS

Territory

Type: Mating, nesting, feeding
Size: Several acres
Main behavior: Song, chases, patrolling
Duration: From arrival of male through breeding phase

Males return in late winter or early spring to areas where they bred the previous year. As soon as they arrive, males start patrolling: circling about the periphery of their territories. While patrolling they may forage silently; or forage, giving the Chirp-call every time they land; or stop foraging and sing. These behaviors can be seen and heard throughout the day. The Phoebe is very conspicuous at this stage, so it is a good time to locate territories where you can follow the birds through the rest of the breeding cycle.

The territories of Phoebes are usually well dispersed, so there are few interactions between neighbors. Most interactions occur early in the season as birds are arriving. The most common response to an intruder is merely to chase it out of the territory. Occasionally a period of singing may follow these chases. In some cases a flight display may be given over the territory or over an intruder. This involves the bird flying with erratic fluttering flight out over an open area while giving a musical twittering composed of a mixture of the bird's Song and calls. This display is most common in early spring and may be used more by some individuals than others. In the few instances where territories have adjacent borders, two males may participate in Song duels, with each bird answering the Song of the other. Later in the season when the female has arrived, the pair may defend the territory together against intruders.

Territories seem to become established fairly rapidly and with little conflict. Once established, patrolling and singing during the day become infrequent. At the start of the second brood, singing may again occur during the day as territorial activity is slightly increased.

Courtship

Main behavior: Song, morning rendezvous
Duration: From arrival of female until incubation

Females may arrive up to two weeks after the males. The birds seem to form pairs without any noticeable ceremony. Once two birds have paired, the male stops most of his patrolling and singing during the day. He stays in the general vicinity of the female, but if he approaches too close, the female will react aggressively to him, giving the Chirp-call and chasing him briefly.

The only time that the pair regularly come in close contact is during what has been termed the morning rendezvous. Slightly before dawn, the male starts singing at a fairly rapid rate of about thirty times per minute. He is usually perched near a potential nest site. Soon the female, who roosts away from the male, approaches the area and lands several yards away from him. He then stops singing and for the next few minutes makes short flights toward her, each time veering off at the last minute and giving the Chirp-call as he lands. Finally, the male does Flutter-flight over her and attempts to land on her back and copulate. The female may accept the male and mate with him, or she may be aggressive to him. Sometimes the male's initial flights toward the female do not result in copulation attempts but simply dissipate, and both birds begin foraging in the area.

Morning rendezvous may continue for three or more weeks, through the nest-building and into the egg-laying period. Once incubation has started, the female stops coming in response to the male's song, and soon after this his morning singing tapers off. If a male loses his mate, he may resume singing during the day.

Nest-Building

Placement: Under bridges, porches, old sheds, cliffs, or upturned roots. On horizontal or vertical supports
Size: Inside diameter 2½ inches; inside depth 1¾ inches
Materials: Mud, moss, fine grasses, and occasionally a few feathers

Several days before nest-building, the male may Wing-flutter and Chatter-call on or over potential nest sites. In some cases these displays have been observed to take place where the nest was eventually built or even on the nest after it has been started. They are done by the male in view of the female and may function to show the female the available nesting sites in the territory.

The female does all of the nest-building, and although the male may accompany her on collecting trips, he rarely comes closer than ten to twenty-five feet from the nest during the day. Most construction occurs in the early morning. The main materials of mud, grass, and moss are collected nearby, and trips to gather material may be made every one or two minutes. The nest may take from three to thirteen days to complete, the longer times being due to bad weather — sometimes the Phoebe arrives early enough to encounter a late snowstorm. When the nest is partially complete, one member of the pair stays on it at night, most likely the female.

In many cases, Phoebes use old nests of their own species or of Barn Swallows. These are always modified in some way before use. In many cases, the same nest is used for second broods as for the first, but only after some additions of new nest material.

Locating the Nest

WHEN TO LOOK In early to midspring

WHERE TO LOOK In old buildings and sheds or under bridges

BEHAVIORAL CLUES TO NEST LOCATION:

1. Locate the males when they first arrive and get a sense of their territory and likely spots for a nest.

2. Watch for the arrival of the female on the male's territory and follow her movements. She should soon lead you to the nest.

Breeding

Eggs: Average 5 for first brood, 4 for second brood. All white
Incubation: Average 16 days, all by the female
Nestling phase: Average 18 days
Fledgling phase: 2 to 3 weeks

Egg-Laying and Incubation

There may be up to three weeks between completion of the nest and laying of the first egg. Egg-laying is generally done in the early morning and one egg is laid each day until the clutch is complete. Incubation is started just before or after the last egg is laid. The female does all of the incubation and only leaves for short periods. When she leaves, the male has a tendency to perch near the nest for at least part of the time she is away.

Watch for Cowbirds during this period, for about 25 percent of Phoebe nests are parasitized. *See* Cowbird.

Nestling Phase

The young usually hatch within a day of each other. Both the male and female participate in feeding them. The female tends to be more wary when approaching the nest, usually landing near the nest first and then going to it. The male, on the other hand, often lands directly on the nest. The young are sometimes fed by regurgitation for the first few days and then gradually are brought larger and larger foods, mainly insects. The parents forage for much of this food on the ground or among shrubs, as opposed to their usual methods of flycatching. This may, in fact, be a clue to recognizing the nestling phase, just by seeing the behavior of the adults. After about six days the young fill the nest, and during the next few days they often perch on the edge and flap their wings.

Fledgling Phase

The young stay with the parents for up to three weeks after leaving the nest, and their call during this time is a slightly drawn-out "treee." At first they are fed all their food by the parents, but after the first week they gain more independence and feed some on their own. Their separation is gradual until about the third week when, if the young are not yet independent, the parents may be aggressive toward them. During this time the family may range up to about a quarter of a mile from the nest. When the parents start a second brood, the young remain in the general area, and only at the end of summer do they venture farther.

A female may start to remake her nest for the second brood as soon as three days after the young of the first brood have left the nest. She may then start laying eggs one or two days later. This results in the male doing the majority of feeding of the first-brood fledglings. Second broods are most common in early June.

Plumage

DISTINGUISHING THE SEXES There is no way to tell the sexes apart through plumage, but there are some hints through behavior. The female does all nest-building and incubation. The male does most of the singing, but the female can sing, and does on occasion.

DISTINGUISHING JUVENALS FROM ADULTS The back and wings of juvenals are olive brown as opposed to the gray-brown of the adults, and their breast may be more yellow.

MOLTS Phoebes undergo one complete molt per year in August and September before migration.

Seasonal Movement

Phoebes are one of the later birds to migrate south in the fall, often staying into October. The bird winters in the southeastern United States and Mexico and remains solitary and, for the most part, silent, although it has been known to give Song and the Chirp-call.

Eastern Wood Pewee / *Contopus virens*

THE PLAINTIVE SONG OF THE EASTERN WOOD PEWEE IN LATE SPRING IS A sure sign that summer is almost here. This bird arrives when migration is almost over, unlike its relative the Eastern Phoebe, who may arrive when there is still snow on the ground. The male Pewee rests on exposed perches under the forest canopy, alternating Song with brief flights to catch passing insects. Every so often he interrupts his feeding and rises to the top of a tree and sings continuously, possibly to keep other males away or to attract a female.

If you get up very early in the morning, you have a good chance of hearing their Dawn-song. It is like a continuous version of their Song with no pauses between phrases. This singing is done almost every morning by the male during the breeding period, and it may last for up to a half hour on a given morning. Its function is not clear but it may be associated with courtship and calling the female to him. Displays like the Dawn-song also exist in other members of the Flycatcher family.

Pewees are visually inconspicuous but territories can be located through the male's Song. The territories are small so that once you find a pair it is fairly easy to return and find them again to observe their behavior.

The nest is well camouflaged: it is small, placed on a fork of a horizontal branch, and covered with lichens. To find it, locate a pair of Pewees, determine which one is the male through its singing, then follow the movements of the other Pewee. This will be the female and she will soon lead you to the nest.

BEHAVIOR CALENDAR

	TERRITORY	COURTSHIP	NEST-BUILDING	BREEDING	PLUMAGE	SEASONAL MOVEMENT	FLOCK BEHAVIOR
JANUARY							
FEBRUARY							
MARCH							
APRIL						▓	
MAY	▓	▓	▓	▓		▓	
JUNE	▓	▓	▓	▓			
JULY	▓	▓	▓	▓			
AUGUST	▓			▓	▓		
SEPTEMBER					▓	▓	
OCTOBER						▓	
NOVEMBER							
DECEMBER							

DISPLAY GUIDE

Visual Displays

No clearly distinguishable visual displays have been recorded for the Eastern Wood Pewee. Only vague references exist to a type of slow, stalling flight accompanied by the Twitter-call. This seems to occur early in the season.

Auditory Displays

Song

Male   *Sp Su*

High, slurred whistles given in short phrases   *peeahwee peeoh*
with long pauses between phrases. There are
two types of phrases: one with three notes,
starting high, going lower, and ending high,
like "peeahwee," and one starting high and
ending low, like "peeoh." In late summer a
version may be heard that is a simple upward
slurred whistle, like "ahwee."

CONTEXT Heard from first arrival until the
birds migrate south. May be heard at any
time during daylight, often quite continuously throughout the day

Dawn-Song

Male   *Sp Su*

Differs from the Song in that the phrases are
given one right after another with only about
a one-second pause. There is also the addition
of a third phrase distinct in that it consists of
three unslurred, whistled notes. May last a
half hour or more

CONTEXT Given regularly in the earliest morning during the breeding season. Dawn-song may be preceded and/or followed by Song

Chip-Call

Male or Female   *Sp Su F*

A short, soft "chip"

CONTEXT Given in a variety of circumstances; possibly functioning as a contact note, or at times as an alarm note

Twitter-Call

Male or Female   *Sp Su*

A short, rapid series of twittering notes somewhat like the Short-song of an American Goldfinch

CONTEXT Occurs most in the early part of the breeding season and may accompany interactions between males and females; possibly associated with courtship

BEHAVIOR DESCRIPTIONS

Territory

Type: Mating, nesting, feeding
Size: Approximately 2–6 acres
Main behavior: Song
Duration: From arrival of male until end of breeding

As soon as males arrive on their breeding grounds they begin to limit their activities to an area of several acres. Song is continually given throughout the day. While feeding, the bird sings from exposed perches under the forest canopy, shifting to a new perch every ten to fifteen minutes. Occasionally the bird stops feeding and flies to an exposed perch at the top of a high tree, above the forest canopy, and sings for several minutes.

Pewees rarely nest close enough to each other to create territorial aggression between males, but when it does occur, the territory holder and intruder may hover opposite each other and grapple as they flutter to the ground.

If a male is unable to attract a female to an area, he may move on to another location.

Courtship

Main behavior: Chases, Dawn-song
Duration: Unknown

Male and female Pewees seem to pair with little or no ceremony, or at least none that has so far been observed. Females arrive after the males, and once on a territory, a female may be chased by the male in rapid, short flights that weave in and out among the trees. These types of chases are common in birds where the sexes are alike and may result from the male initially treating the female as he would another male intruding on the territory.

The Twitter-call has been heard before, during, and after these chases. Its function is not known. The Dawn-song may also function in relation to the pair. In some other Flycatchers, such as the Phoebe, the Dawn-song functions to call the female to the male for the first time each morning. This may be the case for the Pewee as well.

Nest-Building

Placement: On a horizontal limb, well out from the trunk, 20–60 feet above ground
Size: Inside diameter 1¾ inches; inside depth 1½ inches
Materials: Fine plant stems and fibers tied together with insect or spider silk; nest lined with finer plant materials and covered with lichens

The nest of the Wood Pewee is one of the most beautiful and also one of the most inconspicuous of birds' nests. The female is believed to do all of the building. She usually chooses a fork in a horizontal branch, often one that is already covered with lichens. She makes numerous trips during the day and is often seen wiping her bill back and forth over the nest area, possibly transferring sticky silk to the nest foundation. The nest takes at least five to six days to complete, and during the last days the final touches of lichens are added to the outside. During the nest-building period, the male will continue to sing in the territory and occasionally approach the nest site for brief periods.

Locating the Nest

WHERE TO LOOK In mature deciduous woods

WHEN TO LOOK Late spring through early summer

BEHAVIORAL CLUES TO NEST LOCATION:

1. Listen for the male Song and look for female.
2. Watch the movements of the female.

Breeding

Eggs: 2–4, usually 3. White with irregular brown spots around the larger end
Incubation: 12–13 days, by the female only
Nestling phase: 15–18 days
Fledgling phase: 1–3 weeks or longer
Broods: 1

Egg-Laying and Incubation

A day or two may elapse between the completion of the nest and the laying of the first egg. Eggs are laid one per day until the clutch is complete, at which point the female starts to incubate. She is quite active during this phase, her average period on the nest lasting ten to sixteen minutes. She frequently flies off to a nearby perch to catch insects in the air for a few minutes and then returns to the nest. When the temperature is warmer, her periods off the nest tend to be longer. In most cases the male is not seen near the nest but feeds and sings in other areas of the territory, though some observers have recorded the male coming to the nest and feeding the female.

Nestling Phase

For the first few days after hatching, the young are brooded much of the time, but by the fourth or fifth day this has lessened considerably. Both parents care for the young and make numerous feeding trips throughout the day. Visits are brief, as the parents just alight at the nest rim, place the food in the nestlings' mouths, check for fecal sacs, and then leave. For the first few days the fecal sacs are eaten; after that they are carried away. The young are fairly quiet in the nest and may utter no calls at all. Soon they look as if they are all going to fall out of the nest, it is so small. As they lean out over the rim, you can often spot their yellow beaks and the red lining of their mouths.

Fledgling Phase

During this stage the young follow the parents around and frequently give a buzzing, squeaky call. At the same time, the male gives his Song, especially the version that is a single upward slurred note. The behavior of the birds from near the end of the fledgling phase to the time they migrate is not known.

Plumage

DISTINGUISHING THE SEXES Male and female Wood Pewees are alike in plumage and can only be distinguished by their behavior. The male is believed to be the only one to give the Song, and the female is believed to be the one to do most of the nest-building and all of the incubation.

DISTINGUISHING JUVENALS FROM ADULTS Juvenals are very similar to adults in plumage except that their wingbars are lighter and more distinct than those of the adults.

MOLTS Adults have one complete molt starting in late summer and possibly continuing on after migration. A partial molt may occur in spring but this is not known for sure.

Seasonal Movement

Fall migration to the south starts in late August, and the birds seem to take their time moving, as many are still in the southern states in November. The Eastern Wood Pewee winters in northern South America and in Central America. The birds come north inconspicuously and are one of the latest to arrive on the breeding grounds, starting breeding mostly in May.

Barn Swallow / *Hirundo rustica*

IF YOU SEE BARN SWALLOWS WHEELING ABOUT IN THE AIR OR PERCHING on telephone lines, look for the nearest open shed, barn, or other roofed area and you are very likely to find the birds' nests. Barn Swallows seem to have accepted human structures for their nest sites to the exclusion of any natural locations. Obviously the birds bred before humans were building houses, and it is believed that they then used the walls of caves or cliffs. The lack of suitable nest sites may have contributed to their habit of breeding in colonies. In any case, where you find one pair, you are likely to find others as well.

The nest is built on a horizontal or vertical surface and composed primarily of mud with a few grasses woven in for strength. During nest-building it is fun to watch the birds dive down to the edge of a meadow stream and return to the nest with a mouthful of mud. You may also see the birds flying with feathers in their bills, as these are used for the final lining.

Auditory rather than visual displays are the main ways the birds communicate. The Song of the male is best recognized as a continuous musical twitter interspersed with a second or two of a grating sound. After they first arrive on the breeding ground, males do a great deal of singing both from perches and while in flight. They also may sing as they chase the female as part of their courtship. Seeing two birds perched very near each other at this time is a good indication that they are probably paired. Once paired, they soon build a nest, mate, and lay eggs. Incubation and care for the young are shared by both adults. During breeding there is a lot of activity around the nest, for the parents frequently exchange places during incubation and bring food to the nest every few minutes once the young have hatched.

BEHAVIOR CALENDAR

	TERRITORY	COURTSHIP	NEST-BUILDING	BREEDING	PLUMAGE	SEASONAL MOVEMENT	FLOCK BEHAVIOR
JANUARY							
FEBRUARY							
MARCH							
APRIL		■				■	
MAY	■	■	■	■			
JUNE	■	■	■	■			
JULY	■		■	■			
AUGUST				■		■	
SEPTEMBER					■		
OCTOBER					■		
NOVEMBER							
DECEMBER							

DISPLAY GUIDE

Visual Displays

Visual displays of Barn Swallows are not often seen. Some observers have reported Allo-preening, where one bird of a pair preens the other and vice versa; there have also been reports of Billing, a display where birds inter-lock bills momentarily. Both of these displays are prominent in Tree Swallow courtship (see volume 1) and may be present to a lesser extent in that of Barn Swallows.

Auditory Displays

Song

Male or Female   *Sp Su*

A continuous twitter interspersed about every five seconds with grating notes

CONTEXT Given by males throughout the breeding season, but most prominently during courtship and between broods. Most males sing while perched but may also sing during chases. The female may also give fragments of Song before and after the Whine-call. Young Swallows may start singing within a month of leaving the nest, usually while they are in groups with other young Swallows. *See* Courtship

Chit-Chit-Call

Male or Female   *Sp Su F*

A short, harsh call often given in a rapid series of two or three   *chitchit chitchitchit*

CONTEXT A common call given by birds almost continuously as they feed in a flock over fields. Call may also be used by birds as they approach the nest. A louder version of this call is given at times of possible danger near the nest, such as at your approach.

Whistle-Call

Male or Female   *Sp Su*

A short, clear whistle that can be either loud or soft. May be given in series of two or three
CONTEXT Given between members of a pair either when flying or perched. Sometimes given by lone birds. Often given while birds are perched near the nest site, or while the male chases the female (presumably in courtship). Whistle-calls are also given during the flights of flocks high in the air that may be associated with courtship. *See* Courtship

Stutter-Call

Male or Female   *Sp Su F*

A rapid series of harsh sounds on a constant pitch lasting up to a second or slightly more; often repeated several times
CONTEXT May be given by females just prior to copulation

Whine-Call

Female   *Sp*

An extended, harsh sound on a constant pitch lasting up to a second or slightly more; often repeated several times
CONTEXT May be given by females just prior to copulation

BEHAVIOR DESCRIPTION

Territory

Type: Nesting
Size: Immediate area around nest
Main behavior: Song, chases
Duration: During breeding

Barn Swallows do not establish territories until after pair formation. Their territories seem to extend in a straight line from the nest
to the nearest good perch. Pairs of Barn Swallows nesting in the
same barn seem more or less to respect their neighbors' territories,
but newcomers usually undergo a series of attacks as they un-
knowingly trespass on established territories. Chases, fights, and
Song are used in territory skirmishes.

In many cases, Barn Swallows nest in colonies of as many as
forty or more pairs. These nests are often very close together, in
which case each pair's territory size is much reduced, sometimes to
just the immediate area around the nest.

Courtship

Main behavior: Song, chases, communal flights, copulation
Duration: The few weeks before egg-laying

Male and female Barn Swallows arrive on the breeding ground
together. At first the birds perch separately, then as they begin
courtship, they gradually start to perch in pairs. Birds perched
together are usually paired. Sometimes another bird tries to land
between a perched pair but is chased away.

The initial stages of courtship seem to take place on fences and
telephone lines slightly away from nesting sites. Males do a great
deal of singing while flying or perched, and occasionally engage in
chases of the females. During these chases the male gives Song
and/or the Whistle-call while the female often gives the Stutter-call.

If there are many pairs in the area, they may periodically fly up together and feed for ten to fifteen minutes, then resume interactions around the nesting site. The Chit-chit-call is usually given during these feeding flights. At other times you may see large groups of Swallows circling in the air together and hear them giving the Whistle-call and Song. The flights may go as high as two hundred feet and include Swallows from neighboring areas. The purpose of the flights is unclear, but they occur mostly at the beginning of the season and between the two broods. Some observers believe they are a feature of courtship.

Later stages of courtship tend to occur near the nest and include copulation and possibly Billing and Allo-preening. These latter displays, described under Visual Displays, are not as common in Barn Swallows as they are in Tree Swallows. Just before copulation, the female may give the Whine-call and a few Song fragments. The male will fly over and hover behind her, then land on her back and mate. If the female is not ready to mate she may give the Stutter-call, as the male hovers behind her, and fly off.

Nest-Building

Placement: On horizontal or vertical supports, usually protected from rain, such as in buildings, under bridges, or in rock cavities
Size: Inside diameter 3 inches; inside depth 1–2 inches
Materials: Mud, grasses, horse hair, lined with feathers

A few days after you notice Barn Swallows perched in pairs, they are likely to begin building their nest. Both sexes contribute equally to its construction. Nests built on horizontal surfaces need no additional support; but those built on vertical surfaces need some projection or roughness to which the mud of the nest can adhere. One study found that old mud wasp nests were frequently the starting place for these vertical nests.

In order to build the nest, the birds need to locate an adequate source of mud of just the right consistency. They may travel up to a half mile away for this material. To find one of these sources, simply look for Barn Swallows flying down to the ground, for the birds rarely do this at other times. They will remain on the ground for a minute or so and then fly up and off to their nest site. In ten to fifteen minutes they will probably return for more mud. If you look at where they gather the mud, you will see the area marked with numerous small holes made by the birds as they poked their beaks into the mud several times to get a good load. After a few trips to gather mud, the birds collect other materials for the nest, such as grasses or rootlets. The lining is usually downy feathers of some kind. A few feathers may even be added after the eggs are laid.

Frequently Barn Swallows reuse nests from previous years, but before doing so they add a layer of mud to the rim and inner cup and a new lining of feathers. They may use a particular nest for several years, gradually making it up to a foot high.

When Swallows build their nests under concrete and wooden bridges, they may nest with Phoebes. Both species may use the nest of the other as a starting platform.

Locating the Nest

WHERE TO LOOK In barns, old sheds, or under bridges or docks
WHEN TO LOOK April to May, soon after birds arrive
BEHAVIORAL CLUES TO NEST LOCATION:

1. Look for birds continually going in and out of a building.
2. Follow birds that have collected nesting material.
3. Look in any area where birds are perched.

Breeding

Eggs: Average 5. White spotted with brown
Incubation: 15 days by female and male
Nestling phase: Average 18–20 days
Fledgling phase: About 4 weeks
Broods: 1–2

Egg-Laying and Incubation

Egg-laying begins one to three days after the nest is finished. One egg is laid each day until the clutch is complete. Incubation may start before the last egg is laid, causing hatching to spread over several days. Although the male and female take turns at the nest during the incubation period, it is likely that the male does not perform effective incubation, since he does not have a well-developed incubation patch, and his stints at the nest often involve simply standing over the eggs. The birds change places on the nest about every fifteen minutes, usually giving the Whistle-call or Chit-chit-call as they do so. Some observers have noticed a difference in the behavior of the male and female on the nest. While on the nest, the male is still and generally just watches other birds in the area; the female, to keep the eggs evenly warmed, always rolls the eggs with her beak every time she returns to the nest, no matter how short her absence, and while on the nest she frequently preens and changes position.

During the incubation phase, the female stays on the nest at night and the male either perches near her or flies off and roosts farther away.

Nestling Phase

The young hatch over a period of one to three days and are fed by both parents. Feedings may occur as often as once per minute or as infrequently as every fifteen minutes. The young are fed throughout the day, from the earliest light until after dark. Their food consists mostly of live insects, brought one at a time by the parents.

At first the young are frequently brooded by either parent, but brooding time decreases rapidly after the fourth day. At about the same time, the young begin to stretch their necks, peer over the rim of the nest, and give their first faint peeps, which can be heard from below. At first the parents eat the fecal sacs of the young, but then in a few days they carry them off. About the twelfth day, the young begin to back up to the edge of the nest and defecate out over the rim; before that time the only droppings on the ground below the nest are from the parents. If the nest is on a house or other structure where you don't want the mess of the droppings, simply put a container below the nest, especially for this last stage of the nestling phase.

Fledgling Phase

The young may leave the nest over a period of a day or two. For the first few days they stay fairly near the nest, returning to it or its immediate vicinity to roost. After that they do not return to the nest site. Families seem to stay together for several weeks after leaving the nest. If the parents start another brood, they may stop feeding the young after two weeks, but the young may remain in the area longer.

Often groups of juvenals from first broods gather into flocks and feed and perch together. A month after leaving the nest, the young birds may sing a subsong that contains grating notes like the parents'.

Behavior While Perching in Groups

Swallows often perch side by side along telephone wires, especially at the end of the breeding season. It seems that birds express dominance through interactions at these perching sites. Interactions occur when one bird tries to perch too close to another. In these cases one of three things can happen: the approaching bird may make the perched bird fly away or retreat; the perched bird may display and cause the approaching bird to stop or retreat; or the birds may land near each other and, after displays, remain still.

In the first two cases one bird seems to be dominant over another, but in the last there seems to be a standoff. Dominant birds in interactions point their opened bill toward their neighbor; submissive birds tend to turn their heads away. Some birds may challenge others by sidling toward them along the wire. Juvenals are allowed to come close to adults without aggression. They may even beg from strange adults and peck at their wings and tail without being attacked. Periods of a great deal of auditory displays, mainly Chit-chit-call and Song, alternate with quiet times when all birds preen vigorously.

Plumage

DISTINGUISHING THE SEXES There is no sure way to distinguish male from female through plumage, but generally males have longer tail feathers than females. In terms of behavior, generally only the male sings; although the female can sing, she usually does so only with fragments of Song preceding copulation.

DISTINGUISHING JUVENALS FROM ADULTS Outer tail feathers of juvenals are shorter and more rounded than those of adults, and they extend less than an inch beyond the central tail feathers. MOLTS Barn Swallows undergo one complete molt per year, in late fall and winter, usually after they have migrated south.

Seasonal Movement

In the northern part of the range, the birds start flocking soon after their first brood and start migrating in early August, finishing by the third week in August. In the East, they seem to gather along the coast to feed and roost. They often alternate sitting in large flocks along the beaches with taking to the air to feed. They often seem to fly south on particularly strong south winds. While migrating, they may fly high but more usually remain as close as a few feet from the ground. They migrate by day and possibly by night as well.

The birds migrate north in large flocks sometimes mixed with other species of Swallows. The birds reach the southern edge of the United States in April and can continue migrating through May. The birds heading East seem to fly over the Indies to Florida, while those destined for the West fly up through Central America and Mexico.

Tufted Titmouse / *Parus bicolor*

IN LATE WINTER AND EARLY SPRING, THE LOVELY "PETER PETER" SONG of the male Tufted Titmouse increases in frequency and will easily catch your attention. When you imitate it, it usually brings the caller into sight, as he appears expecting to find a rival male in his territory. The increase in Song signals the start of the breeding season and the breakup of the family flocks that have stayed together throughout winter. Birds that are not already paired will seek mates. Rival males will come together at territorial borders and answer each other's Song. These latter meetings often escalate into more intense aggression, in which the birds do Wing-quiver and give the High-see-call.

Once paired, Tufted Titmice remain close together. As they move about, they keep in aural contact with each other by means of their soft Tseep-call. The male often feeds the female, and she solicits food from him by giving the See-jwee-call or the High-see-call accompanied by Wing-quiver. Mate-feeding continues through the nest-building and incubation phases and is a marvelous part of Titmouse behavior to watch.

The nest is built in an existing tree cavity. The female does most of the building and often collects large amounts of moss or bark. During the nestling phase, the parents signal their approach to the nest with a soft version of Song. Late in the nestling phase you can imitate this Song near the nest and the young will readily answer with their calls from the nest.

BEHAVIOR CALENDAR

	TERRITORY	COURTSHIP	NEST-BUILDING	BREEDING	PLUMAGE	SEASONAL MOVEMENT	FLOCK BEHAVIOR
JANUARY							▓
FEBRUARY							▓
MARCH	▓	▓					
APRIL	▓	▓	▓	▓			
MAY	▓	▓	▓	▓			
JUNE	▓			▓			
JULY							▓
AUGUST					▓		▓
SEPTEMBER							▓
OCTOBER							▓
NOVEMBER							▓
DECEMBER							▓

DISPLAY GUIDE

Visual Displays

Head-Forward

Male or Female   *Sp Su F W*

Bird assumes a horizontal posture and may lunge toward another bird. Bill may be open and wings slightly spread.

CALL None

CONTEXT Given in aggressive encounters (may be seen at feeders)

Wing-Quiver

Male or Female   *Sp Su F*

Bird opens wings out to the side, slightly or quite a lot, and quivers them. Bird may be crouched.

CALL High-see call

CONTEXT Given by males in aggressive encounters with other males, by females and males before mating, by females during mate-feeding, and by fledglings when being fed. May also be given by adults when they bring food to the nest. *See* Territory, Courtship, Breeding

Crest-Raise

Male or Female   *Sp Su F W*

Crest of bird is held erect.

CONTEXT Given in situations of disturbance or alarm

Song

Male or Female   *Sp Su F W*

peeyer peeyer or
peeto peeto or
peter peter

A clear, whistled phrase containing two notes either slurred or unslurred. Phrase is repeated in succession two or more times.

CONTEXT Occurs at any time of year but is most frequent during breeding. Given primarily by males when forming territory or advertising for a mate. A softer version is given by male or female when approaching the nest with food. *See* Territory, Courtship, Breeding

See-Jwee-Call

Male or Female   *Sp Su F W*

tseejwee tseejwee

A short, two-part call; the first part is high and squeaky, the second lower and more rasping. There are several variations.

CONTEXT Given mostly in aggressive encounters with other Titmice. Occasionally given by the female during mate-feeding. A variable version given by the fledglings when they get food from the adults

Jway-Call

Male or Female   *Sp Su F W*

jwayjwayjway or
jweejweejwee

A harsh, scolding note with a rasping quality; given repeatedly

CONTEXT Given in aggressive encounters or in moments of alarm

High-See-Call

Male or Female   *Sp Su*

An extremely high-pitched, whistled note   *seeeseeeseeeseee*
given in a rapid series

CONTEXT Given by males in conflicts over
territory. Given by males and females before or during copulation. Given by female
during mate-feeding. *See* Territory,
Courtship

Tseep-Call

Male or Female   *Sp Su F W*

A short, soft, single-note call

CONTEXT: A short-distance contact note
given by members of a pair as they move
about. *See* Courtship

NOTE: Tufted Titmice have an amazing variety of whistling and rasping calls. The ones
listed here are among the most common.

BEHAVIOR DESCRIPTIONS

Territory

Type: Mating, nesting, feeding
Size: Approximately 2–5 acres
Main behavior: Song, chases, High-see-call, Wing-quiver
Duration: From late winter until the end of breeding

Family groups often stay in loose flocks with other family groups
through the winter. The flocks range in an area of approximately
fifteen to twenty acres. In later winter and early spring there is a
gradual breakup of the flocks into pairs and lone birds. This
breakup may be accompanied by much chasing and aggression.

Both paired and unpaired males begin to sing throughout the day from prominent perches in their respective territories. A singing male often attracts a neighbor to a common border and the two may come quite close, each answering the Song of the other. When near each other, Song may be replaced by the Jway-call. The males may separate after calling or the conflict may intensify, with one or both birds giving the High-see-call and doing Wing-quiver or flying in short circular flights around each other. Sometimes the birds even lock feet and fall to the ground in a fight. The intensity of conflicts increases as nesting approaches.

Courtship

Main behavior: Mate-feeding, chases, copulation
Duration: From late winter through the incubation phase

There are some curious features to the courtship of Tufted Titmice. One is that pairs may form at any time of year. Another is that there are no displays during initial pair formation, except possibly chases, but there are a number of displays given between the pair once they have joined. Males seem to be dominant over females throughout the year; they will often fly at females and chase them about. These chases may figure prominently in pair formation and be the earliest stage of courtship. Once paired, male and female always stay together, often using the Tseep-call to stay in contact.

Mate-feeding is prominent in the behavior of Titmice in late winter and spring. Prior to the birds' mate-feeding, your attentioin will most likely be attracted by the female as she gives the See-jwee-call or the High-see-call with Wing-quivering. She may follow the male closely about or she may remain at a distance and display intensely. During this time the male seems to search for food at a faster than normal pace, maybe because he is collecting food for both himself and her. When he finds food he may eat it or fly to her and place it in her beak.

Copulation in Titmice is often seen. It is made conspicuous by both the male and female giving the High-see-call. The call may occur before and during copulation. Wing-quiver is done by the female and occasionally by the male as well.

Nest-Building

Placement: 3–90 feet up in tree cavities, birdhouses
Size: Nest hole at least 1½ inches in diameter
Materials: Leaves, moss, cotton, wool, bark strips, hair (occasionally plucked from animals and humans)

The pair first explore all available nest cavities. After choosing one, the female builds the nest. She carries large mouthfuls of material each trip, usually starting with leaves and moss and bark, then adding fine material, such as hair. It takes six to eleven days to build the nest. The female may add material to the nest during incubation and up to the second day before hatching. The male remains near and frequently mate-feeds the female. Copulation also takes place during the nest-building phase.

Nest hole above with portion cut away to show eggs

Locating the Nest
WHERE TO LOOK In wooded areas or swampy areas
WHEN TO LOOK March through May

1. Listen for the High-see-call that accompanies mate-feeding and copulation since these take place near the nest.

2. Watch for Titmice making trips with nest material in their bills or gathering it from the ground, since they collect material near the nest.

3. Listen for calls of nestlings coming from the nest.

Breeding

Eggs: 4–8, average 5–6. White, speckled with small brown dots
Incubation: 13–14 days by female only
Nestling phase: 17–18 days
Fledgling phase: 4 or more weeks
Broods: 1–2

Egg-Laying and Incubation

The eggs are laid one each day until the clutch is complete. When she leaves the nest during the egg-laying phase, the female generally covers the eggs with nest material. Also, throughout most of egg-laying and incubation she may continue to bring material into the nest. Incubation starts after the last egg is laid. During incubation the female's average period on the nest is thirty to forty minutes, and her average period off the nest is ten to twenty minutes.

Mate-feeding continues through the incubation phase. At first the male comes to the nest area and gives Song; the female comes off the nest and takes the food. She may then return to the nest or go off with the male to feed some more. Later in the incubation phase the male sings and comes to the nest entrance, where the female receives the food. Both birds may Wing-quiver during mate-feeding and you may hear the High-see-call or See-jwee-call.

Nestling Phase

The young hatch over a one- to two-day period. The female carries out the eggshells from within the nest. The female broods the young for the first few days and is the one that stays on the nest at night throughout the nestling phase. Both parents feed the young and as they approach the nest usually give a soft version of Song. As the young get older, they start giving their own calls when they hear the Song of the parents. At this stage it is easy to get the young to start calling from within the nest simply by imitating the Song of the adults. The young leave the nest when they are seventeen or eighteen days old.

In a few cases, birds from first broods have been observed bringing food to the young of the second brood.

Fledgling Phase

After they first leave the nest, the young follow the parents around, giving loud See-jwee-calls. This is a very conspicuous time in the birds' life cycle, for the noisy juvenals can be heard easily in the woods. They may continue to get food from the parents for four or more weeks after leaving the nest.

The young remain with the parents through the winter. They are believed to leave their parents in late winter and early spring, when territorial and courtship activities begin.

Plumage

DISTINGUISHING THE SEXES Male and female Titmice are identical in plumage, so behavior must be observed to tell them apart. The male is the main one to give loud, clear Song in spring, although females can sing. During mate-feeding, the male feeds the female. Also, the female is the one that builds the nest and incubates the eggs.

DISTINGUISHING JUVENALS FROM ADULTS The best clue is the gray forehead of the juvenals; adults have a black forehead patch. The juvenals also have a lighter and less prominent buff on the sides of their bellies.

MOLTS The birds have one complete molt per year, in August.

Seasonal Movement

Titmice do not migrate but instead form small flocks and remain in the winter in a fixed "range" of about fifteen to twenty acres. At the end of winter, there may be movement and breakup of these flocks. Some Titmice may stay in the same area from year to year; others may leave. Some young may disperse and breed near where they were born; others go farther away.

Flock Behavior

Titmice gather into small flocks in the winter. These are probably composed of family members: parents and siblings from the last breeding season. They may stay remarkably close together all winter. Occasionally these flocks may join with Chickadees, Downy Woodpeckers, and Nuthatches, but this is only a temporary association. Birds keep in contact by means of Tseep-calls. Song can be heard all year but increases in frequency in late winter when the flock disperses and territorial behavior begins.

Feeder Behavior

Tufted Titmice remain in family groups in the winter and are conspicuous and vocal at feeders. Many of their displays can be seen, particularly in late winter as flocks break up and courtship begins. Song increases until by midspring it is almost incessant. *See* Display Guide, Territory, and Courtship.

COMMON DISPLAYS Song, Head-forward, Crest-raise, and most calls. Males are dominant over females at the feeder.

OTHER DISPLAYS If you hear the High-see-call near the feeder, look for the birds; you may see mate-feeding and copulation. The High-see-call and Wing-quiver may also be used by males that are being aggressive to one another. Titmice will bring their fledglings to feeders, and the fledglings will beg noisily from the parents.

White-Breasted Nuthatch/*Sitta carolinensis*

NUTHATCHES ARE BEST KNOWN FOR THEIR HABIT OF STORING FOOD IN bark crevices and their curious ability to move headfirst down trees. The birds often move along trunks and branches in a jerking, zigzag motion giving them the comical appearance of a mechanical windup toy.

They are excellent birds for the behavior-watcher, for there is a close relation between the pair throughout the year, and active courtship begins in late winter, long before most other birds. On some cold January morning, often at the crack of dawn, you may see and hear the male Nuthatch do his early courtship display. In a full performance, he perches at the top of a tree, gives his loud "werwerwer" Song, and bows his body down with each note. In many cases, the female soon arrives and the pair go off and feed together for the day, keeping in aural contact through soft Ip-calls.

A prominent feature of the later stages of their courtship is mate-feeding. The male collects a morsel of food, often one that has been stored in a special place, and carries it to the female. The female usually sits still on a perch while the male lands near her, runs straight to her, rather than in the usual zigzag manner, and places the food in her bill. Mate-feeding can frequently be seen if you follow the birds about. It continues into April.

The birds nest in existing tree cavities, often where a knothole has been rotted out. In many cases they have to compete with squirrels and other nest-hole birds for these holes. Each bird also has a hole in which it roosts during winter; you have a good chance of finding its roost if you follow a bird on a winter evening and see it enter just as it begins to get dark.

BEHAVIOR CALENDAR

	TERRITORY	COURTSHIP	NEST-BUILDING	BREEDING	PLUMAGE	SEASONAL MOVEMENT	FLOCK BEHAVIOR
JANUARY	█						
FEBRUARY	█	█					
MARCH	█	█					
APRIL	█		█	█			
MAY	█		█	█			
JUNE	█		█	█			
JULY	█			█	█		
AUGUST	█						
SEPTEMBER	█						
OCTOBER	█						
NOVEMBER	█						
DECEMBER	█						

DISPLAY GUIDE

Visual Displays

Song-Bow

Male   *W Sp*

While singing from an exposed perch, the male extends his neck and bobs his head and body with each repetition of Song. Between Songs the bird may sway from side to side.

CALL Song

CONTEXT Usually occurs in relation to female. May be used in her presence or while he is calling her to him. *See* Courtship

Tail-Fan-Back-Ruffle

Male or Female   *Sp Su F W*

Tail is raised and wings are drooped. Tail may be fanned, back feathers may be ruffled, and head may point down.

CALL None

CONTEXT Occurs in conflicts with other birds. The variations of Tail-fan-back-ruffle may in fact be separate displays. Further study is needed before they can be clearly defined. *See* Territory

Wing-Spread

Male or Female   *Sp Su F W*

Body and bill are pointed vertically, wings and tail are fully spread, and bird sways slowly from side to side. It may last only one or two seconds or it may be longer.

CALL None

CONTEXT Given near the nest or near a feeder when bird is competing with other birds or mammals

Song

Male   *Sp Su F W*

werwerwerwer
werwerwer

A rapid series of eight to eleven notes given in a two- or three-second period. In spring it may be repeated regularly for long periods of time.

CONTEXT Given by male from conspicuous perches, often at the tops of trees. Combined with the visual display of Song-bow when the female is near. Song may also be given while the male is feeding, and in these cases it probably acts as a long-distance contact note.

Ank-Call

Male or Female   *Sp Su F W*

ank, ank or
ankank or
a'a'a'a'a'

A loud, nasal call given either singly, in twos, or in a long, rapid series

CONTEXT When given singly it is most often a contact note; when double it usually denotes a mild disturbance or excitement; when in a long, rapid series, it means extreme excitement, usually conflicts with other pairs of Nuthatches. *See* Courtship, Territory

Ip-Call

Male or Female   *Sp Su F W*

ip. ip. or *it. it.*

A soft, slight note given in irregular rhythm and often alternately between two birds

CONTEXT Given between members of a pair as a contact note as they move about and feed. Male and female may have slightly different pitches.

Pheeoo-Call
Male or Female   *W Sp*

A wheezy whistle, first rising and then falling in pitch. Not like any other Nuthatch call

CONTEXT Given in what seem to be moments of intense excitement between members of a pair. May be given by male just before his short chases of the female during court-ship. *See* Courtship

Fledgling-Call
Male or Female   *Su*

Short, squeaky calls often repeated

CONTEXT Given by the young during the fledgling phase, especially when they are begging for food from the parents. Wing-quivering may accompany the calling.

BEHAVIOR DESCRIPTIONS

Territory

Type: Nesting, feeding, mating
Size: 25–45 acres
Main behavior: Ank-call, Tail-fan-back-ruffle, chases, Wing-spread
Duration: Throughout the year

White-breasted Nuthatches remain within a fairly fixed range throughout the year, but during breeding they claim a smaller portion of this range for a territory. Conflicts with other birds over territory occur primarily in winter and spring. One of the most conspicuous displays associated with these conflicts is the Ank-call given in a rapid series. This is usually loud and easily heard. Go to the area of the calling and you are likely to see two pairs of birds (for distinguishing the sexes, see Plumage). The birds will be feeding about the trees, and every so often one bird will fly at another, usually of its own sex. You may also hear the softer Ip-calls given between members of each pair. Usually these interactions dissipate after a few minutes as each pair moves off into its own territory. If the conflicts are more intense, another display may be seen: the Tail-fan-back-ruffle. Sometimes one bird may use a swooping flight over another while creating a whirring sound with its wings.

Another aspect of behavior that may be territorial is the spring singing of males. Sometimes Song is alternated between two males, creating what seems to be a Song duel, possibly making males aware of each other's territorial borders.

Since Nuthatches remain in one area throughout the year, they are more used to their neighbors and there is less cause for territorial defense. The territories being so large, it is common for a pair to wander briefly onto another's territory while feeding and then move back. In fact, in some cases, ranges of birds overlap and the two pairs may be seen feeding in the same area.

A feeder at the edge of a territory may be used by more than one pair. If it is in the center of a territory, the resident pair may keep other pairs away.

Courtship

Main behavior: Mate-feeding, Song, chases
Duration: January through April

Nuthatch pairs remain together in the same area throughout the year. How closely the pair associate varies with the seasons, from fall when each bird is quite independent, to spring when they are in close synchrony. The reestablishing of their closeness starts in January and February. You will recognize it by the sight of the male and female staying within fifty feet of each other, keeping in contact with the steady use of the Ip-call. Ip-calls seem to be a close-distance contact call, while the double Ank-call is often used for keeping contact over slightly greater distances.

At the time when the pair are reestablishing their closeness, the male will begin singing from the tops of trees early in the morning. The singing is often accompanied by Song-bow. In many cases a female may show up after he has sung for a while, and the two may go off and feed together, using just the Ip-call and Ank-call. Or the male may just continue to sing, with the female resting motionless near him. Song may also be heard when the male and female are feeding far apart, and in this case it may function as a long-distance contact call.

One of the most prominent features of Nuthatch courtship is mate-feeding. Starting in late winter and continuing into the breeding phase, the male will be seen flying to the female and giving her bits of food. Sometimes you can get a sense of when a male is going to mate-feed, for he seems to become more active in his movements while searching for food. In some cases, he may go to a particular spot, clearly to retrieve a stored piece of food. Usually the female receives food with little or no display, but the male's behavior may vary. He may run along a branch in a straight line to the female rather than in the usual zigzag hitching. Sometimes the food in the male's beak is not taken by the female, in which case he may store it in a bark crevice or he may peck it apart and then return and give it to the female. Mate-feeding increases in frequency as nest-building and egg-laying approach. Once the young hatch, it soon stops.

Occasionally a third bird will interact with a pair: a female chasing another female in the presence of her mate, or two males swooping at one another. These may be lone birds vying for one member of a pair. The conflicts are often followed by renewed display between the original pair, such as increased Ip-call, Song, or mate-feeding.

An unusual auditory display of Nuthatches is the Pheeoo-call. This is given by both birds in situations of what appear to be high sexual motivation. In early winter you may hear the call from the male as he moves excitedly about the female and possibly even chases her. The female gives the Pheeoo-call before and after copulation.

Nest-Building

Placement: 5–50 feet off the ground in a natural tree cavity, old wood-
pecker hole, or birdhouse
Size: Minimum opening of 1½ inches in diameter but often seems to prefer
holes 2 or 3 times that size
Materials: Bark, grasses, rootlets, fur

White-breasted Nuthatches most often nest in the rotted knotholes of large trees. Usually the pair are in close association during nest-building, both giving the Ip-call frequently, the male occasionally feeding the female, and the two staying close to the nest while actively flying about. The female seems to do most of the building. You can often get quite close and watch the female collecting materials from the ground or off trees. Trips are frequent and nest-building can be seen at most times of day, especially morning and late afternoon.

You may see the birds sweeping their bills back and forth over the bark near the nest hole. This bill-sweeping can continue for ten minutes or more and occur several days in a row. In some cases the birds have crushed insects in their bills and then wiped their bills on the bark. At other times you may see bits of fur stuffed in bark crevices all about the nest hole. It has been suggested that these activities leave a scent that deters squirrels and other mammal predators from the nest area. Bill-sweeping most often occurs before and after periods of nest-building, but it can also be seen, especially in late afternoon, during the incubation and nestling periods.

Squirrels and birds such as Titmice, Starlings, and House Sparrows may compete for the nest holes chosen by Nuthatches. Often these competitions result in the Nuthatch being routed, but not until after it has fought and displayed for a considerable period. One display that might be seen during interspecies encounters is the Wing-spread. The bird will sway slowly back and forth or wobble slightly in this display; sometimes it even momentarily hangs underneath a branch in this pose.

Throughout the year each bird spends the night in a separate roost hole. Each morning as the birds leave, they carry away any feces that may have been ejected during the night. Sometimes a female takes over a male roost hole in late winter and early spring, and that hole may become the nest hole for the breeding season. In winter it is possible to follow birds to their roost holes, just by watching their movements at sunset.

Nest hole above with portion cut away to show eggs

Locating the Nest

WHERE TO LOOK In deciduous woods where there are older trees with rotted holes in them

WHEN TO LOOK In early spring

BEHAVIORAL CLUES TO NEST LOCATION:

1. Mate-feeding, especially in spring, is often done near the nest hole.

2. Watch for the female gathering any nest material and follow her.

Breeding

Eggs: 5–10. White with light brown dots concentrated at larger end
Incubation: 12 days by female only
Nestling phase: About 14 days
Fledgling phase: About 2 weeks

Egg-Laying and Incubation

The eggs are laid one per day until the clutch is complete, and incubation starts with the laying of the last egg. Once incubation has started, the female spends long periods on the nest, but if you watch for a while you are very likely to hear the male approach, give the double Ank-call, and then go to the nest hole and feed the female. He feeds her a great deal through this period. Occasionally she may leave the nest and feed with the male, both birds giving the soft Ip-calls as they move about together.

One other activity is storing food. Both birds come to the nest tree and store bits of food in bark crevices near the nest. This can be retrieved later and used in self-feeding, mate-feeding, or feeding the young. You may see another Nuthatch foreign to the pair come near the nest hole and steal some of this stored food.

Nestling Phase

The young are likely to be brooded for the first few days after hatching, and during this time the male will bring food both for the young and the female. At times she leaves the nest and gathers food for herself and the young. Fecal sacs are removed from the nest. After about a week you can begin to hear the calls of the young. They are repeated, short, high-pitched squeaky sounds and can be heard at first about fifteen feet away, later from slightly farther. The calls are given most when the parents arrive. If you are too close to the nest, the parents may give a rapid Ank-call until you move farther back, but in general you can watch them from twenty to thirty feet away.

Fledgling Phase

The young may receive food from the parents for about two weeks after leaving the nest, but the family remains together as a group for much longer. Occasionally they may be seen together even into fall, at which time the young presumably disperse.

Plumage

DISTINGUISHING THE SEXES Males and females can be distinguished, with practice, by looking at the dark patch on top of their heads. In the male this patch is jet black, while in the female it is lighter and has a silvery sheen to it. The sexes can also be distinguished through behavior, for the female builds most of the nest and does all incubation, while the male sings and brings food to the female during mate-feeding.

DISTINGUISHING JUVENALS FROM ADULTS Juvenals look very similar to adults, but their feathers will be fresher, especially on the white breast, and will not be worn down like those of the adults from their constant movement in and out of the nest hole. Male and female juvenals can be distinguished by their head patch, just like the adults.

MOLTS Adult Nuthatches have one complete molt per year, in late summer.

Seasonal Movement

Most Nuthatches are year-round residents in the area where they breed. But there is also clearly a section of the population that migrates slightly or wanders to areas of better food availability. These latter birds may be mostly immatures.

Feeder Behavior

Nuthatches are endearing to watch as they comically hitch their way around trees. Most of their auditory and visual displays can be seen at or near your feeder. You may have several pairs, for the winter ranges of Nuthatches can overlap. You can tell males from females (see Plumage) and you can even come to recognize individual females, for their head patterns vary from pale silver to dark gray. See Display Guide, Territory, and Courtship.

MOST COMMON DISPLAYS The pair keep in contact through their soft Ip-calls. Listen for Ank-calls, particularly rapid Ank-calls, for they indicate mounting excitement, and look to see if the birds are doing the Tail-fan-back-ruffle display.

OTHER DISPLAYS In late winter and early spring, males may begin giving Song from the treetops near your feeders. Another display given by Nuthatches around feeders, particularly to squirrels and chipmunks, is the Wing-spread display.

John Gill

Marsh Wren / *Cistothorus palustris*

MALE MARSH WRENS HAVE A MARVELOUS LITTLE DISPLAY THAT THEY frequently do over their territories. They fly up five to fifteen feet, well above the reeds and cattails they live in, and then flutter gradually down, all the while giving their dry, rattling Song. The display is called Song-flight and it is a great help in locating the males and seeing the extent of their territories. The territories are usually only a quarter acre in size and often many are grouped together.

While forming his territory, the male also builds a number of nests. When the female arrives she chooses one and adds the final lining to it or builds one of her own. It is usually not too hard to spot one or two of the nests. They are spherical, woven from cattail and grass leaves, and have a small entrance on the side. They are about the size of a softball.

An interesting feature of these birds is that, in many cases, the males are polygamous. Two females per male is the most common, and these females usually nest at opposite ends of the male's territory. Their breeding phases are most often staggered a week or two apart.

Marsh Wrens are very closely tied to the particular environment of cattail or Spartina marshes. Where these habitats abound, so do the birds. Where the habitat is scarce or not large enough, the birds are rarely seen.

BEHAVIOR CALENDAR

	TERRITORY	COURTSHIP	NEST-BUILDING	BREEDING	PLUMAGE	SEASONAL MOVEMENT	FLOCK BEHAVIOR
JANUARY							
FEBRUARY							
MARCH					▓		
APRIL	▓	▓	▓			▓	
MAY	▓	▓	▓	▓		▓	
JUNE	▓	▓	▓	▓			
JULY	▓	▓	▓	▓			
AUGUST	▓	▓	▓	▓	▓		
SEPTEMBER					▓	▓	
OCTOBER						▓	
NOVEMBER							
DECEMBER							

DISPLAY GUIDE

Visual Displays

Song-Flight

Male   *Sp Su*

Bird flies up five to fifteen feet and then gradually flutters down at an angle. Flight is very fluttery.

CALL Song

CONTEXT Done by male over territory. *See* Territory

Fluff-Out

Male   *Sp Su*

Bird fluffs breast feathers and cocks tail up. Wings may be quivered and bird may sway from side to side.

CALL None or Song

CONTEXT Used at borders of territories by neighboring males, and by the male near a female when she is looking at courting nests. *See* Territory, Courtship

Auditory Displays

Song

Male   *Sp Su*

A dry, rattling warble. Song is repeated frequently and each bird can give many versions of it. Between songs birds may give a low "whirring" sound.

CONTEXT Used in territorial advertisement and in attracting a mate. *See* Territory, Courtship

Chek-Call

Male or Female   *Sp Su F W*

A short, harsh, low-pitched call. May be given in a rapid series, producing a chatterlike call. CONTEXT Given by birds when there is any cause for alarm

BEHAVIOR DESCRIPTIONS

Territory

Type: Mating, nesting, feeding
Size: ⅛ to ⅜ of an acre
Main behavior: Song, Song-flight, chases, nest-building
Duration: From arrival of male on breeding ground until end of breeding

As you approach a cattail marsh, you are likely to hear Marsh Wrens long before you see them. Males arrive on the breeding ground ahead of the females. Song is an important feature of their territorial behavior and is given during much of the day and as frequently as ten to fifteen times per minute. The typical behavior of a territorial male is to sing from one side of his territory for a few minutes, then fly to the other side and sing there for a while. Every so often he will launch himself five to fifteen feet in the air and then gradually flutter down to another spot giving Song as he does so. This is the Song-flight display.

Territories are small and frequently border each other. Neighboring males may countersing back and forth across a common border. Each male has many versions of his Song, and some studies have suggested that neighbors may try to match each other's Songs—the dominant bird initiates the changes and the subordinate bird tries to match them. Two males within sight of each other may do the Fluff-out display, sing, or chase one another.

During this period of territory formation, males are also engaged in making "courting nests," and since they may construct several of these (*see* Courtship), as well as defend territory, this is a very active time for them.

If an arriving female settles in an area between territories, the neighboring males will all try to expand their boundaries to include her. This may be how some males become polygamous. The territories of polygamous males are larger than those of monogamous males who are in the same habitat.

In certain areas of the country, Wrens do not migrate, and in the winter the males have loosely defined territories. As spring approaches, singing rates increase and boundaries become more defined.

Courtship

Main behavior: Building courting nests, Song
Duration: From arrival of female through nest-building

As an important part of their courtship, male Marsh Wrens build a number of "courting nests" to attract females. These may look like finished nests from the outside, but they consist of just an outer shell of woven cattails and do not have any of the inner layers of a finished nest. The nests may be clustered in one part of the territory, or they may be spread out if the territory is small. Most Song takes place in this "courting center," and foraging usually takes place elsewhere with little singing. When a female arrives, she will go around to several males' nests and inspect them. A male follows her, sings rapidly, and does the Fluff-out display. Pairing takes place when the female accepts one of his nests and adds a lining to it. In some cases the female may build a new nest with little or no help from the male.

When the female first arrives at the marsh, she is not yet sexually ready for mating and, if pressed by the male, may wedge herself in the cattails and hiss at him. She becomes ready for copulation during nest construction. At this time, the male may sing and do the Fluff-out display, and she may perch on a cattail and rapidly vibrate her wings with her bill up and tail tilted over her back. The male will then climb up on her back while rapidly fluttering his wings and copulation will take place. Afterward, both may remain quietly in the area for a short while.

Marsh Wrens often are polygamous, with two, and on rare occasions three, females paired with one male. Rates of polygamy vary from as low as 3 percent in some areas to 50 percent in others. Extra females tend to join males who have territories in thick cattail stands even though there may be available bachelors with territories in more sparsely vegetated areas.

Most males try to become polygamous and will start building more courting nests and singing to attract another mate around the time their first mates are ready to start egg-laying. The first female stays in a fairly small area during breeding, and in the thick vegetation she may not see or come into contact with the second mate of the male, if he gets one. Should the females come into contact with one another, there may be fights.

Nest-Building

Placement: In cattails or reeds 1–3 feet high
Size: 7 inches high; 3 inches wide
Materials: Cattail leaves, reeds, grasses, lined with cattail down, feathers, rootlets

When male wrens arrive on their territory, they begin building a number of "courting," or dummy, nests. These are incomplete nests that consist of an outer shell of woven cattails, grasses, or sedges. They may build as many as twenty-seven nests but average five or six. It takes one to three days to complete a nest and the male may work on several at once. He lashes together the supporting plants to make a foundation on which the nest rests. Grasses, some of which may be water-soaked, are woven around to make the nest. Some leaves of the supporting structure are woven in as well. On the side, about a third of the way from the top, there is an opening about one and a quarter inches in diameter.

When the females arrive and become paired, they select one of the male's nests and add the lining, or they may build a new nest of their own with very little help from the male. Inside the nest the female makes a lining of grass and sedge leaves, then adds wet cattail fluff, which dries and makes a tight, insulating layer, and finally a layer of fine grass or sedge strips. Feathers may also be added. In this nest there is a door-step-like projection that leads from the outside of the nest to the inner chamber.

The courting nests of the male may be used in other ways, such as by adults to roost at night, by fledglings for shelter after they leave the breeding nest, and in winter by adults where there is a resident population.

Locating the Nest

WHERE TO LOOK In marshes with reeds or cattails

WHEN TO LOOK As soon as the males arrive on the breeding ground and start singing

BEHAVIORAL CLUES TO NEST LOCATION:

    1. In areas where the male is singing, look for a woven globe of material among the cattail leaves or reeds.

Breeding

Eggs: 3–8. Cinnamon brown with darker spots
Incubation: 13–15 days, by female only
Nestling phase: 14–16 days
Fledgling phase: About 2 weeks
Broods: 1–2

Egg-Laying and Incubation

Occurs anytime between early April and mid-August. Eggs are laid one per day, and egg-laying usually begins the day after the nest is complete. The female begins incubation before the last egg is laid, and eggs hatch in the order in which they were laid. Only the female incubates. When it is hot, she may spend less time sitting on the eggs. While she is incubating, the male spends his time away from the nest, building new courting nests, singing, and attempting to get another female.

Nestling Phase

Hatching may take place over two days. The female removes the eggshells from the nest. Both males and females feed the young, but in some cases males only feed the young from later broods. The female may brood the young until they are seven or eight days old. Both parents remove fecal sacs, but later in the nestling phase the young back up to the nest opening and defecate. The young leave the nest fourteen to sixteen days after hatching. When there are two broods, a new nest is built, and this may be started one to four weeks after the young have left the first nest.

Fledgling Phase

The young may stay together as a group during the fledgling stage. They follow after the parents with loud begging calls. During the first night or two, they may return to the breeding nest to roost, or they may stay in one of the male's courting nests. The young are fed for twelve or more days. They usually remain close to the breeding nest until independent. At the end of summer, the young birds form flocks. Sometimes as many as twenty-five or thirty move about together, feeding near the water's edge.

Plumage

DISTINGUISHING THE SEXES The sexes are alike in plumage. In behavior, only the male does Song and Song-flight. The female is the only one to incubate the eggs.

DISTINGUISHING JUVENALS FROM ADULTS Juvenals are very similar to adults except their eye stripe is less distinct and in some cases almost lacking.

MOLTS Marsh Wrens have two molts per year: a complete molt in late summer and a partial molt in spring.

Seasonal Movement

In the west and south Marsh Wrens may be permanent residents. In other areas where migration does occur, it takes place gradually. The first birds to leave are the adults and young from first broods. They migrate in late August and early September. The birds that migrate later are mostly the young from second broods that are still completing their fall molt. Most of these migrate from mid-September to mid-October.

Marsh Wrens winter along the southern and western coasts and in the southern states and Central America. The birds migrate north from late April into early June. The first birds to migrate are the older males, then older females, then younger males and younger females.

Brown Thrasher / *Toxostoma rufum*

THE BROWN THRASHER, ALONG WITH THE MOCKINGBIRD AND GRAY Catbird, is a member of the family Mimidae. All of these birds share the interesting feature of endlessly improvising their Song, often mimicking the auditory display of other birds. They have no one Song of their own. A good way to sort them out is to remember that, in general, Catbirds repeat phrases once, Brown Thrashers twice, and Mockingbirds three or more times.

When Brown Thrashers first arrive in spring, it is by far the easiest time to watch them, for the male sings loudly from tree-tops in his attempt to attract a female. Once paired, the birds are much harder to observe, since the male gives only a soft version of Song from concealed perches, and the two carry out most of their activities in dense thickets and shrubbery. The pair move quietly about their territory, staying close together as they feed on the ground. In the Midwest and South where there is a dense Thrasher population, they may nest more commonly around buildings, parks, and other human habitats, and are more frequently seen.

Their nest is similar to that of the Catbird and Mockingbird, as it is large, composed primarily of sticks with a rootlet lining, and well hidden in dense cover. In fact, you can be several feet from the nest and not know it, especially when the female is incubating, for she will wait until the very last minute before flushing, relying heavily on her colors blending with the surroundings.

BEHAVIOR CALENDAR

	TERRITORY	COURTSHIP	NEST-BUILDING	BREEDING	PLUMAGE	SEASONAL MOVEMENT	FLOCK BEHAVIOR
JANUARY							
FEBRUARY							
MARCH							
APRIL	▓	▓	▓	▓		▓	
MAY	▓	▓	▓	▓		▓	
JUNE	▓	▓	▓	▓			
JULY	▓	▓	▓	▓			
AUGUST							
SEPTEMBER					▓		
OCTOBER						▓	
NOVEMBER							
DECEMBER							

DISPLAY GUIDE

Visual Displays

Wing-Flutter
Female   *Sp*
Female approaches male, fluttering her wings
and chirping. She may also pick up and carry
a twig in her beak
CONTEXT Courtship

Auditory Displays

Song
Male   *Sp Su F*
A long series of short, musical phrases, often
given in pairs. May include phrases from
other birds' Songs.

Examples:
*teeahwee teeahwee,
teeoo teeoo, chay
chay,* etc.

CONTEXT Given during the breeding season
from a short time after the males arrive to
the beginning of nest-building. Once nest-
building starts, only a soft, whispered version of Song is given. At the start of a
second brood, Song may again be loud. *See*
Territory, Courtship

Smack-Call
Male or Female   *Sp Su*
A one-note call that sounds like a loud kiss
CONTEXT Given in situations of alarm

Teea-Call
Male or Female   *Sp Su*
A harsh note that rises in pitch as it is rapidly
repeated
CONTEXT Given as an alarm when the young
are threatened

BEHAVIOR DESCRIPTIONS

Territory

Type: Mating, nesting, feeding
Size: 2–10 acres
Main behavior: Song, chases
Duration of defense: From the arrival of the male to the end of breeding

Male Brown Thrashers arrive on the breeding ground ahead of the females. For the first few days they may not sing. In areas where the population is sparse, males will give Song loudly from the tops of trees and roam over a large area. If a male then attracts a mate, the two of them will confine their movements to a smaller area and start to build a nest.

In areas where there are many Thrashers, territories may border on each other. In these cases, males immediately form smaller territories with clear boundaries. Territories are advertised through the male's Song and borders are clarified by chases between neighbors.

Once mated, males use a softer version of Song during territorial encounters.

Courtship

Main behavior: Quieter Song of the male; the pair staying close together
Duration: For the week or two before nest-building

There are very few signs of courtship and pair formation in Brown Thrashers. The female seems to arrive on the male's territory with few or no displays. Pairing may take place rather quickly, and a sign that it has occurred is that the male no longer gives his Song loudly from exposed perches. Instead, he only gives a very soft, whispered version of Song from lower perches in concealed areas. He remains close to the female and the two move about the territory foraging and exploring nesting sites. If the two are separated, the male may sing a little more loudly.

During copulation, the female rapidly quivers her wings and gives a repeated, high-pitched note. Before or after copulation, one or both birds may pick up and drop bits of leaves and twigs.

Nest-Building

Placement: On the ground under thickets, or in shrubs or trees; up to 15 feet off the ground, average 2–7 feet
Size: Outside diameter 12 inches; inside depth 1 inch; inside diameter 3¾ inches
Materials: Twigs, dry leaves, grass, grape bark, rootlets

Both birds help select the nest site. While collecting nest material they hop about on the ground, picking up bits and dropping them. Sometimes they pull twigs down from branches above them. All of this seems to be a testing of materials. The male may sing softly while this is going on. Both male and female carry material to the nest and both may deposit it in the nest, but the female seems to be the one who does most of the nest shaping.

The nest is composed of four layers. The first layer is of twigs, some of which can be a foot or more long. The second layer is made mostly of dead leaves. Sometimes grape bark or paper is added here too. The third layer is made up of small stems, twigs, and roots, but the roots still have the dirt on them, unlike the fourth and last layer, the lining, which is made of cleaned rootlets. The Thrashers may collect these from living grasses and beat them against the ground to remove the dirt.

Locating the Nest

WHERE TO LOOK In thickets and dense, tangled shrubbery

WHEN TO LOOK From early spring on

BEHAVIORAL CLUES TO NEST LOCATION:

1. Listen for the male singing and try to get a sense of his territory.

2. Look for a pair carrying or collecting nesting material and follow them.

3. The male may sing quietly from a perch near the nest.

Breeding

Eggs: 4 or 5 usually, can be 3–6. White, sometimes covered with fine red dots

Incubation: 12–14 days by male and female

Nestling phase: 9–12 days

Fledgling phase: Unknown

Broods: 1–2

Egg-Laying and Incubation

Eggs are usually laid early in the morning. Both birds incubate, but the female may do more than the male. The male is more restless on the nest than the female and more easily frightened off. The female is very still on the nest and you can approach within a foot or two of her. The male may sing early in the morning while he is on the nest. Both birds turn the eggs while they incubate. Some observers have seen the male feeding the female away from the nest.

Nestling Phase

Brooding is done by both parents and is fairly continuous during the first few days of the nestling phase. Both parents also feed the young. After feeding a nestling, the parent will wait until it defecates and then remove the fecal sac. The parent eats the fecal sacs for the first half of the nestling phase and after that carries them away.

Sometimes Thrashers can be very protective of their young and are known to fly at human intruders and give the Smack-call or Teea-call.

Fledgling Phase

After the young leave the nest, they remain nearby in concealed spots and are fed by the parents. If the first nest has been successful and there is time, the female will begin to build a second nest by herself a few days into the fledgling phase. The male will then continue to care for the fledglings of the first brood. If there is no second brood, the parents may divide up the care of the young and even move with them to separate areas.

Plumage

DISTINGUISHING THE SEXES Adult male and female Brown Thrashers are identical in plumage and also have very similar behavior. Practically the only behavioral trait that separates the two is that the male gives Song and the female doesn't.

DISTINGUISHING JUVENALS FROM ADULTS Eye color differs: juvenals have a gray iris, adults a bright yellow.

MOLTS The birds undergo one complete molt per year, in late summer.

Seasonal Movement

Thrashers in southern states are permanent residents, while those in the north migrate in September and October. The birds remain in the Gulf states through the winter, usually staying well concealed in thickets near wet areas. In April they move north to their breeding grounds.

Wood Thrush / *Hylocichla mustelina*

THE FLUTELIKE PHRASES OF THE WOOD THRUSH SONG PERMEATE AND seem to blend into the wet, shaded woods where the birds breed. In this habitat where sight lines are limited, auditory displays become the most important means of communication. Males give Song frequently, especially in the morning and early evening. Females give shorter versions of Song when there is a disturbance near the nest. Both sexes use the Bweebeeb-call and Bwubub-call, which can be given at various intensities, generally in response to some disturbance, although occasionally they may function as contact notes when given softly.

The nest of the Wood Thrush is very similar to that of the Robin and shows the relationship between the two birds. It is composed of grasses, with an inner lining of mud and finer grasses. It is usually placed on a fork of a horizontal limb and often close enough to the ground that one can see the activities of the birds.

The rufous coloring of the Wood Thrush is certainly a spectacular feature of the bird. Its Spread display accentuates the bird's spotted breast. This display is done in aggressive interactions concerning territory. The bird flattens and laterally expands its breast feathers and laterally compresses its head feathers. From the front the bird looks as if it has a fat breast and thin head. Two other visual displays to look for are the obvious Wing/tail-flick and the more subtle Crest-raise.

BEHAVIOR CALENDAR

	TERRITORY	COURTSHIP	NEST-BUILDING	BREEDING	PLUMAGE	SEASONAL MOVEMENT	FLOCK BEHAVIOR
JANUARY							
FEBRUARY							
MARCH							
APRIL	▓	▓				▓	
MAY	▓	▓	▓	▓		▓	
JUNE	▓	▓	▓	▓			
JULY	▓	▓	▓	▓	▓		
AUGUST				▓	▓		
SEPTEMBER						▓	
OCTOBER						▓	
NOVEMBER							
DECEMBER							

DISPLAY GUIDE

Visual Displays

Wing/Tail-Flick

Male or Female *Sp Su F*

The bird gives repeated rapid flicks of its tail and/or wings. The crest may also be raised and lowered repeatedly.

CALL Bwubub-call

CONTEXT A common display given by birds that are mildly disturbed, as when you approach their nesting area. *See* Territory

Spread

Male or Female *Sp Su F*

Breast feathers are spread laterally, making chest look broad, while head feathers are compressed laterally, making the head look thin. Crest, back, and rump feathers may be slightly fluffed. Wings are drooped and the bird sits erect on its perch. May be accompanied by Wing/tail-flick.

CALLS Bwubub-call, Bweebeeb-call, or Song

CONTEXT Given in times of extreme excitement while facing the source of the disturbance. Increased spreading of breast feathers indicates greater excitement. May be given toward other bird species as well. *See* Territory

Crest-Raise

Male or Female *Sp Su F*

The bird quickly raises its crest feathers and then slowly lowers them.

CALL None or Bwubub-call

CONTEXT This display may accompany other displays, such as Spread or Wing/tail-flick. Given during moments of slight disturbance. *See* Territory

Horizontal-Fluff

Male or Female   Sp Su F

The bird, while in a horizontal posture, fluffs its breast and back feathers and compresses its head feathers. The bill is usually open (gaped).

CALL None

CONTEXT A short-distance aggressive display, usually done while perched near another bird of the same or other species. *See* Territory

Auditory Displays

Song

Male or Female   Sp Su F

bupbup eeeohlay, bupbup ahohlee

A short sequence of flutelike notes rising and falling, often preceded by a series of lower repeated notes. Sometimes just fragments of Song may be given.

CONTEXT Given mostly by males, from their first arrival on the territory until late in the season. Song usually starts at daybreak or earlier, is only sporadic during the day, and then becomes more continuous from about sunset until dark. Evening Song may be more common late in the breeding season. Short versions of Song given by female during territory defense. *See* Territory, Courtship

Bwubub-Call

Male or Female   *Sp Su*

A low, murmuring call of three to five   *bwububububub*
syllables

CONTEXT A common call, given as a contact
note between mates and also as a low-
intensity alarm call, especially in the pre-
nestling stage. *See* Territory

Bweebeeb-Call

Male or Female   *Sp Su*

A moderately loud and excited call, of about   *bweebeebeebeebeeb*
four or five syllables, distinguished from the
Bwubub-call by its loudness, higher pitch,
and *e* or *i* sound. Varies in character with
changes in intensity. May intergrade with
Bwubub-call

CONTEXT Given during aggressive interactions and in situations of medium- and
high-intensity alarm, such as the approach
of a predator or human. More frequent
during nestling and fledgling phase. *See*
Territory

Eee-call

Male or Female   *Sp Su*

A high, squeaky whistle

CONTEXT The context is not clear, but the call
has been noted frequently during the nestling phase, possibly helping adults coordinate activities about the nest.

Fledgling-Calls

Male or Female   *Su*

A short, high "chip" that at later stages may

be uttered in twos or threes. Another call is a rapid series of squeaky notes.

CONTEXT The chip is given from a day or two before they leave the nest to the end of the fledgling phase. Possibly a contact note to help the parents locate them. The other call is given just as the birds receive food from their parents. *See* Breeding

BEHAVIOR DESCRIPTIONS

Territory

Type: Mating, nesting, feeding
Size: ¼–2 acres
Main behavior: Song, chases, Crest-raise, Wing/tail-flick, Spread
Duration of defense: From male's arrival on breeding ground until end of breeding

The first melodic songs of the male Wood Thrush are a good sign that the bird has arrived on its territory. Wood Thrushes usually return to the same territory from year to year. Their territory ranges in size from a quarter of an acre to two acres, the larger sizes often being among human settlements. Song is especially common in the earliest morning and the evening, while only sporadic during the day. The first week after arrival, the males sing from high, exposed perches but later may switch to lower, more concealed sites.

Interactions between males over territory include chases and a variety of displays. Most often intruding males are simply chased out of a territory by the owner. Before, during, or after these chases, you are likely to hear and see several displays. Visual displays, listed in order of increasing intensity, are Crest-raise, Wing/tail-flick, and Spread. The last is perhaps the most spectacular of the three. In this, the bird faces his opponent and laterally spreads his breast feathers. The feathers can be spread just a little or a great deal, depending on the intensity. Calls include the Bwubub-call and, with greater alarm, the Bweebeeb-call.

Song duels are a common territorial interaction between males. In these, two males approach to within about ten yards of each other and alternate Songs. When they are within sight of each other, they may do the Spread as well.

During the nestling and fledgling stages especially, the female may also join in defense of the territory, using Spread along with Bwubub-call and Bweebeeb-call. At this time she may also give short fragments of Song.

The Horizontal-fluff is generally used only in situations where two birds are suddenly near each other, such as while perched during a brief interlude in a chase.

Wood Thrushes are occasionally aggressive to other species in their territories, such as Robins, Jays, and Grackles, and use many of the same displays to oust them.

Courtship

Main behavior: Chases, Song
Duration: For a week or two after arrival of female

Females arrive on the breeding grounds a few days after the males. Upon entering a male's territory they are chased by the male in the same way he would chase an intruding male. The difference in these chases is that the female, even when being chased, stays within the male's territory, rather than fleeing. This results in roughly circular chases and a high level of hostility in both birds. A striking feature of this time is the increased loud singing of the male, possibly as a result of his increased aggression. This, in turn, may in some way further stimulate the female to remain.

The chases continue for several days, gradually decreasing in intensity until they are merely leisurely, short-distance flights with the male following the female. This latter type of chase, which is usually done close to the ground, may continue into the egg-laying phase.

Some observers have noted the use of an "eeee" call during these chases; others have seen the birds pause during the chases and feed together on fresh leaves.

Copulation usually takes place near the nest but is not often seen.

Nest-Building

Placement: Generally 5–20 feet high and on a horizontal limb where there is a fork of branches to help support it
Size: Inside diameter about 3½ inches; inside depth about 2 inches
Materials: Long, dead grass, paper, and string form the foundation, then dead leaves, then mud and a lining of rootlets

Before nest-building begins, you may see two types of behavior: the male carrying long nesting material in front of the female and stopping in spots that are suitable nest sites; or the female crouching down and "molding" (turning around) in spots where a nest could be built. Following these, the female will build the nest. It may be completed in three to five days, with the most intensive work being done on the second and third days. The female may build at any time from sunrise to sunset, with a lull in midafternoon. Various behaviors of the male may occur during this period, including singing infrequently, chasing the female, perching near the nest, and possibly even molding a little. He may also accompany the female on some of her trips to gather material, or he may feed fledglings when the female is building a nest for a second brood.

Locating the Nest

WHERE TO LOOK In moist areas of deciduous woods where there is an understory of shrubs

WHEN TO LOOK Soon after the female arrives in April and May

BEHAVIORAL CLUES TO NEST LOCATION:

1. Locate a territory by listening to the male's Song.
2. Watch for the female carrying nesting material.
3. Listen for Bwubub-call or Bweebeeb-call, which will be given by the birds as an alarm call as you get near the nest site.

Breeding

Eggs: 2–5. Blue green, unspotted
Incubation: 12–13 days by the female only
Nestling phase: 12–14 days
Fledgling phase: About 2 weeks
Broods: 1–2

Egg-Laying and Incubation

Egg-laying starts one to three days after the completion of the nest. The eggs are laid one per day until the clutch is complete. The larger clutches of four or five eggs tend to be the early ones; later clutches are smaller, with two or three eggs. The female does all of the incubation and usually starts just before the laying of the last egg, although roosting on the nest may start right after the laying of the first egg. The female is remarkably attentive, spending 80 to 90 percent of the time at the nest. Depending on the temperature, she either sits on the eggs or stands next to them on the rim of the nest. When sitting, she occasionally gets up to shift the position of the eggs with her bill or she may just turn and change her position on the nest, facing another way. Her average attentive spell is thirty minutes, and her average spell away from the nest is seven minutes.

While the female is incubating, the most common behavior of the male is to perch in one of several trees twenty to thirty yards from the nest and feed, sing, or preen. When the female leaves the nest, the male flies to the nest and perches near or on it, occasionally singing. It is unusual for the male not to come to the nest while the female is away. However, if there is a second brood, the male is often involved with feeding the fledglings from the first brood and so is not as attentive at the nest of the second brood.

Nestling Phase
The young may hatch over a period of one to three days. During the nestling phase the female broods or attends (stands at the nest edge) her young about 70 percent of the time. The male does about two-thirds of the feeding of the nestlings, and feedings may average every six or seven minutes. When the female leaves to feed, she usually returns with food for the young as well. During her absence, the male may stay for part of the time at the nest. In the first days, feces are generally eaten, usually by the female, who is brooding while the male goes off for more food.

Fledgling Phase
When the young first leave the nest, they remain in the territory but scattered about it, up to fifty yards from each other. After they can fly and do some feeding on their own, they are more likely to follow one of the parents. With first broods, both the male and female feed the fledglings. If there is a second brood, the male

cares for the fledglings from the first brood while the female starts laying eggs for her second brood.

For the last brood of the season, both male and female feed the young, and each parent continually associates with certain fledglings. The young gradually leave the area of the adults in two to three weeks.

Plumage

DISTINGUISHING THE SEXES There is no way to distinguish male from female by appearance; however, there are marked sexual differences in behavior. Most of the time it is only the male that sings, and usually it is only the female that builds the nest and incubates and broods the young.

DISTINGUISHING JUVENALS FROM ADULTS Juvenals have brown caps and upper backs dotted or streaked with buff, while adults have clear rusty-red caps and upper backs.

MOLTS There is one complete molt per year, at the end of July and through August.

Seasonal Movement

Wood Thrushes start their fall migration in October and have completed it by November. They seem to travel in flocks for at least part of the time and often fly at night. The birds winter in Mexico and Central America and sometimes on the Caribbean Islands. The male is known to sing in winter. The birds remain on their winter grounds singly.

Wood Thrushes first appear in the United States in late March and are fully migrating in April. By mid-May they have reached the northernmost part of their range — the Great Lakes and southern Canada.

Cedar Waxwing / *Bombycilla cedrorum*

THE CEDAR WAXWING IS ONE OF OUR LOVELIEST BIRDS, ITS COLORS SO blended and feathers so sleeked, it has the appearance of a skill-fully painted carving. The birds are most often seen in flocks as they drift down into a berry patch, perch in a fruit-laden tree, or fly out over a stream to catch insects. In fact, the flock is a central feature of Cedar Waxwing behavior. Even during breeding they will leave their nest to feed with the flock when they hear the Seee-call of other Waxwings flying overhead. When these flocks return from feeding, various pairs separate into their respective nesting territories.

Pairing takes place in the migrating flocks, so if you see a flock, look for the birds doing their curious Side-Hop display. In this the male hops toward a prospective mate with a berry in his beak. She may then take the berry, hop away, then back, and pass the berry to him. This hopping and passing continues until one of them eats the berry. The display occurs in late winter and spring.

At first all Waxwing calls may sound similar, but with a little patient listening you can learn to discriminate among them and they will be a useful clue to the stage of their breeding cycle (see Display Guide). They are also one of the best clues to locating the birds.

Cedar Waxwings can have two broods, and it's not unusual to find their active nests in September or October.

BEHAVIOR CALENDAR

	TERRITORY	COURTSHIP	NEST-BUILDING	BREEDING	PLUMAGE	SEASONAL MOVEMENT	FLOCK BEHAVIOR
JANUARY							▓
FEBRUARY							▓
MARCH		▓				▓	▓
APRIL		▓				▓	▓
MAY	▓	▓	▓			▓	
JUNE	▓	▓	▓	▓			
JULY	▓	▓	▓	▓			
AUGUST	▓	▓	▓	▓			
SEPTEMBER	▓	▓	▓	▓	▓		
OCTOBER				▓	▓	▓	▓
NOVEMBER						▓	▓
DECEMBER						▓	▓

DISPLAY GUIDE

Visual Displays

Side-Hop

Male or Female   *Sp Su*

A Waxwing with food in its bill hops sideways toward another Waxwing and passes the food to it. The other Waxwing hops away, then toward the first bird, and passes the food back. One of the birds may bow between hops. Display is repeated until one bird eats the food.

CALL None

CONTEXT Side-hop is an important part of courtship. It takes place between two birds when they are in a flock or alone. It is initiated by males and functions to identify a female as a prospective mate. When done to another male, that male may respond with Head-forward. When done to a female, she may leave, join him in the display, or seemingly make no response. May be preceded or followed by fast circular flights between the pair. *See* Courtship

Head-Forward

Male or Female   *Sp Su F W*

Body is horizontal, feathers slightly fluffed, crest raised, bill gaped. Bill may be repeatedly snapped.

CALL None

CONTEXT An aggressive display given toward other Cedar Waxwings and sometimes other species of birds. *See* Courtship

Wing-Rowing
Female or Fledglings   *Su F*
Bird lifts wings and moves them in a circular, rowing motion.
CALL **Bzee-zee-call**
CONTEXT Given by female or by fledglings when they receive food from the male or parents respectively. *See* Courtship, Breeding

Auditory Displays

Seee-Call
Male or Female   *Sp Su F W*
A drawn-out, very high pitched, hissing whistle

seeeee seeeee   CONTEXT This is the most commonly heard Waxwing call. It is given by members of a flock as they fly or land, by birds while feeding, and by members of a pair when they are near the nest. *See* Territory, Courtship, Breeding, Social Behavior

Bzee-Call
Male or Female   *Sp Su*
bzeeee bzeeee   Similar to Seee-call but distinctly buzzy and shorter. May also be slightly louder and lower pitched then Seee-call. Irregularly repeated
CONTEXT Given between members of a pair during circular flights around nest and during nest-building. *See* Courtship

Bzee-zee-Call
Female or Fledglings   *Su F*
bzeezeezeezee   Like the Bzee-call but given in continuous
bzeezeezee   rapid series

CONTEXT Given by the female when she receives food from the male and by fledglings when they are receiving food from the adults. Can sound similar to the repeated chirps of a field cricket. *See* Courtship, Breeding

Tseeah-Call

Male or Female   *Su F*

A high, thin whistle, distinguished from the   *tseeeaah tseeeaah*
Seee-call by its marked downward slur at
the end

CONTEXT An alarm call given when there is some possible danger near the nest. *See* Breeding

BEHAVIOR DESCRIPTIONS

Territory

Type: Nesting (mating)
Size: ⅛ to 1 acre
Main behavior: Guarding, chases
Duration of defense: From start of nest-building until end of last nestling phase

For Waxwings, pair formation takes place within the migrating flock, so the birds are already paired before they arrive on the breeding ground. Territory formation is fairly uncomplicated: the birds pick a nesting spot and defend the area immediately around it as they begin to build.

An important feature of the territory is the male's guarding perch. This is a prominent perch from which the male watches for intruders and gives the Seee-call to keep in touch with the female. If an intruder is spotted, the male may do the Head-forward display and dive down at it. Both the male and female will drive intruders out of the territory.

The only activities that take place solely in the territory are incubation and feeding of the nestlings. To feed, the birds leave the territory, join with other Waxwings, and go to areas where there is a plentiful supply of berries or insects. They then return to their separate territories, pairs often avoiding the territories of others on their way back. Mating may take place in or outside the territory.

Often, several pairs of Waxwings will nest near each other, and nests can be as close as twenty-five feet. The same territory may be used for second broods.

Courtship

Main behavior: Side-hop, chases, Bzee-call, mate-feeding, Bzee-zee-call
Duration: Spring through breeding

The first phase of courtship for the Cedar Waxwing, the Side-hop display, takes place in migrating flocks and continues up until incubation. A male will sidle up to a female, who is usually perched facing in the same direction as he, hop sideways, and pass her a berry or piece of fruit that he has collected. She will accept it, hop away, then hop back to him, passing the berry again. This hopping and passing may last up to fifteen minutes, ending when one of the birds eats the berry. Side-hop may be preceded or followed by rapid circular chases between the members of the pair. These circular chases often occur when the birds rejoin after being separate for a while. The Bzee-call usually accompanies the chases.

Copulation almost always is preceded by Side-hop. After the birds have hopped back and forth several times, the female crouches down and may vibrate her wings. The male immediately hops up on her back, his crest raised, and mates.

When the egg-laying starts, Side-hop and the circular chases diminish. Mate-feeding is prominent in this second phase of court-ship. The female, on or near the nest, crouches, does Wing-rowing, and gives the Bzee-zee-call. During this time the female may actively follow the male around. Mate-feeding continues through the incubation phase.

An interesting change takes place when the eggs hatch. When the male comes to the nest, he feeds the female first, then both birds feed the young.

Nest-Building

Placement: 4–50 feet high in fork of a horizontal limb, usually well out from trunk
Size: 3–3¼ inches inside diameter; 1–1¾ inches inside depth
Materials: String, twigs, yarn, rootlets, grass, stems, rags, paper, pine needles. Nests may be lined with moss, grasses or caterpillar silk

During courtship the pair may explore suitable limb forks, finally choosing one. The male and female both build the nest. A common call during nest-building is the Bzee-call. The birds do not work continuously, but intersperse building with feeding, resting, and courting. The most building occurs in the morning and late afternoon. The nest is completed in three to nine days, the average time being six days. Waxwings will often be seen taking material from other birds' nests and using it for their own. They also regularly use old webbing from tent caterpillar and fall webworm nests.

Locating the Nest

WHERE TO LOOK In bushes or trees near open areas

WHEN TO LOOK Soon after the birds arrive to late summer and early fall

BEHAVIORAL CLUES TO NEST LOCATION:

1. Watch for two birds hopping around a tree inspecting limb forks.

2. Listen for Bzee-call; this is given by members of a pair when nest-building.

3. Watch for birds repeatedly making straight flights out of one spot in a tree. Waxwings are indirect about going to the nest, often alighting in lower branches and making a short series of flights up to nest, but they always leave the nest with a direct flight.

Breeding

Eggs: 2–6, may lay fewer eggs in late-season broods. Pale gray with a few brown spots
Incubation: 12–14 days by female only
Nestling phase: 15 days
Fledgling phase: 6–10 days
Broods: 1–2

Egg-Laying and Incubation

Eggs are laid early in the morning on consecutive days, and incubation may start before the last egg is laid. During egg-laying, some additional material may be added to the nest. Only the female incubates, and her periods on the nest are most commonly twenty to forty minutes. While incubating, she may give a very soft warbling call, inaudible over fifteen feet away, and she may give the Seee-call as she leaves and returns to the nest. During incubation, the male remains within sight of the nest and makes frequent trips to feed the female, regurgitating berries that he has collected, while the female does Wing-rowing and gives the Bzee-zee-call.

Nestling Phase

Hatching may extend over a two-day period. The female often eats the discarded shells. When the male now comes to the nest, he usually feeds the female first and then both birds feed the nestlings. For the first two days, the young are fed insects; after that they are fed berries. The female broods the young almost constantly for three days. After that her brooding time diminishes, and when the young are about five days old, she starts making feeding trips. Both parents eat the fecal sacs of the young until about the tenth day, when the young are able to back up to the edge of the nest and defecate over the rim. When about eleven days old, the young will answer calls of their parents and may bill-gape when they hear other Waxwings fly overhead.

Waxwings usually have a second brood, and many of the activities of renesting are interspersed with caring for the first brood. When the nestlings are seven days old, the female may resume courtship behavior. As she prepares to lay a second clutch, the activities of the male may reach a peak as he feeds the fledglings, courts the female, and starts building the second nest. The female will assist more in building the nest as the time of egg-laying draws near. The first egg is laid in the second nest just about the time the birds of the first nest have fledged. Because of this overlap, Waxwings can successfully raise two broods in an average of sixty-five days.

Fledgling Phase

The young maintain close contact with their parents for up to three days after leaving the nest. The parents feed them, stay near the nest, and at night roost close by. After this, the young begin to feed themselves more. Their first flights are unsteady and they have difficulty landing until about the sixth day, when they become more proficient. The young are fed by the parents up to ten days after leaving the nest. Following this, they join other juvenals and feed in small flocks.

Plumage

DISTINGUISHING THE SEXES There is no way to distinguish the sexes by plumage. Even behavior does not give a lot of clues to the sexes. The main ones are that the female incubates, and during mate-feeding she is the one that gives the Bzee-zee-call and does Wing-rowing. See also Side-hop in the Display Guide for responses of males and females to this display.

DISTINGUISHING JUVENALS FROM ADULTS The juvenals have light brown streaking on a gray-brown breast; adults have no streaking on the breast. Juvenals also have more white on the face and lack the black mask and chin patch of the adults.

MOLTS The birds undergo one complete molt per year, in September and October.

Seasonal Movement

The movement patterns of Waxwings in winter are far from clear. Some birds seem to migrate south in fall and into winter. There are many records of Waxwings arriving in Central America as late as January or February. Some of these same birds do not leave to migrate north until April or May. It is also clear that some flocks of Waxwings remain north all winter, where they roam about erratically, possibly because of the shifting availability of food.

In spring, many observers have noted two waves of flights. The first occurs in January and February when large flocks appear in northern states. These flocks seem restless and move about constantly. By early spring they have moved on, and following them are smaller flocks that seem to be the ones that breed in the area.

Flock Behavior

Waxwings are highly social birds and feed in flocks throughout the year. Only during the brief breeding period do they vary from this and spend part of each day in the nest area raising the brood, but even then they will occasionally leave to feed for a while with other Waxwings. The main call of birds in a flock is the Seee-call, which seems to be used endlessly as the birds fly, land, and feed.

Yellow Warbler / *Dendroica petechia*

YELLOW WARBLERS ARE CHARMING LITTLE BIRDS THAT ARE EASILY watched as they move about their small territories. Males in neighboring territories often interact with Circling, a flight display where a male circles out toward another male and then returns.

Their nest is one of the most beautiful to be seen. It is made primarily of downy fibers, such as the dispersal filaments of willow seeds. The female is particularly obvious during nest-building, for she usually makes frequent trips across open areas with this white fluff in her beak. You may also see her go to the nests of tent caterpillars and gather bits of their webbing to use to help bind the fluffy material together. The nest site is easy to find at this time. The nest is usually placed quite low so that you have a good chance of looking right into it and seeing the eggs and the young as they develop.

An interesting feature of Yellow Warblers is that the male has two distinct versions of Song and each version seems to be given in different contexts. One version has an accented ending, the other an unaccented ending. Although there is still some controversy about their meaning, the former version seems to be used more often in relationship to the female, while the latter is more often in relationship to other males. Listen for these two versions of Song and observe for yourself what their context seems to be.

BEHAVIOR CALENDAR

	TERRITORY	COURTSHIP	NEST-BUILDING	BREEDING	PLUMAGE	SEASONAL MOVEMENT	FLOCK BEHAVIOR
JANUARY							
FEBRUARY							
MARCH					▓		
APRIL	▓	▓			▓	▓	
MAY	▓	▓	▓	▓			
JUNE	▓	▓	▓	▓			
JULY	▓			▓	▓		
AUGUST						▓	
SEPTEMBER							
OCTOBER							
NOVEMBER							
DECEMBER							

DISPLAY GUIDE

Visual Displays

Circling
Male   Sp Su

The bird flies out toward another male and then circles back. The other male may then do the same in response.

CALL None

CONTEXT Done by males early in the season. Helps establish territorial boundaries. *See* Territory

Gliding
Male   Sp Su

With wings and tail widely spread, the bird glides in the air.

CALL None

CONTEXT Usually given as the bird glides back into the heart of its territory and away from a neighboring bird. Occurs during territorial conflicts. *See* Territory

Tail/Wing-Spread
Male   Sp Su

The bird, while perched, momentarily spreads its tail and/or wings.

CALL None

CONTEXT Occurs during territorial conflicts, and possibly in courtship. *See* Territory, Courtship

Moth-Flight
Male   Sp Su

The bird flies with a slow, stalling flight with

wingbeats at about twice the normal speed.

CALL None

CONTEXT Occurs during territorial conflicts and in courtship. *See* Territory, Courtship

Auditory Displays

Song

Male   *Sp Su*

A. *sweetsweet-sweeterthansweet*
B. *sweetsweet-sweetsweeswee*

A series of three or four high-pitched, sibilant notes, immediately followed by a shorter, more rapid cluster of similar notes. The only melodic vocalization of the species; sometimes sounds similar to Goldfinch Song. There are two forms: one with an accented ending and one with an unaccented ending.

CONTEXT Accented-ending Songs are given primarily in the presence of the female and during encounters with other, neighboring warbler species. Unaccented-ending Songs are given primarily during encounters with other male Yellow Warblers. *See* Territory

Chip-Call

Male or Female   *Sp Su F W*

A short, rasping "chip"

CONTEXT Given in situations of mild alarm. May be contact call as well

Metallic-Chip

Male or Female   *Sp Su F W*

A short, sharp, metallic sound

CONTEXT Given in situations of extreme alarm

Titi-Call

Male or Female   *Sp Su*

A rapid series of short "chips." The only call   *titititititi*
other than Song that is an extended series
CONTEXT Occurs following long territorial
conflicts

Zeeep-Call

Male or Female   *Sp Su*

A high, sibilant, slightly drawn out note
CONTEXT May be given just before or during
flight. Often heard in fall or late summer
during migration. May function as a contact
call as well

BEHAVIOR DESCRIPTIONS

Territory

Type: Mating, nesting, feeding
Size: ½–3 acres
Main behavior: Song, Circling, chases
Duration of defense: From arrival of male until end of breeding

Males arrive a few days before the females and establish territories by singing from several exposed perches. Males that intrude are chased out. At borders, Circling occurs frequently. In
Circling, one male flies out toward a neighbor and then circles back
into his own territory. The neighbor may then do the same.
Interspersed with chases and Circling may be Gliding and/or
Moth-flights. All of these help to establish a male on his territory.
Following any of these interactions, you may see Tail/Wing-
spread.

Song is a major feature of Yellow Warbler behavior. During
territorial encounters with other Yellow Warblers, the unaccented

version of the Song is the one most frequently given. But Yellow Warblers may also have territorial conflicts with other species of warblers, such as the Chestnut-sided Warbler. In these cases, the accented-ending Song is used along with occasional chases.

Yellow Warbler territories consist of low, shrubby growth occasionally mixed with grassland and often near water. Usually there are some taller objects (up to forty-five feet) in the area from which the male sings and surveys his territory. In areas where no singing posts are available, there seems to be more chasing between males and more encroaching on neighboring territories. It may be that a lack of singing posts makes it harder for the birds to define territories through Song, and therefore more chases occur. In particularly favorable areas, territories may be as small as half an acre; in less favorable areas, they may be as large as two to three acres.

The birds may not always stay right in the territory. If there is not enough food in the area, they may leave and travel up to a quarter of a mile to feed. The birds usually leave their territory with high flights, but when returning usually fly lower. On these lower returning flights they may be attacked by owners of territories they have to cross.

The female does not defend the larger territory and may not even stay strictly within its borders, but she does defend a smaller area in the immediate vicinity of the nest. Once breeding is completed, the birds leave the territory quickly.

There is some evidence that Yellow Warblers are territorial on their wintering grounds in Central and South America. This is especially true of adults, immature birds having a greater tendency to flock at this time.

Courtship

Main behavior: Chases
Duration: Several days after female arrives

Not too much is known about courtship in this species. Females arrive at the territory a few days after the males. A male's first response to a female on his territory is to chase her. But instead of leaving the territory, as an intruding male would do, she remains in it, so the chases between the pair are roughly circular. The chases diminish in intensity and finally stop within two to four days. Males may use Moth-flight and Tail/Wing-spread during interactions with the female. Once the pair become accustomed to each other, they may use the Zeeep-call or Chip-call to keep in contact. Copulation occurs near the end of nest-building, which starts soon after the female arrives.

Nest-Building

Placement: In the upright fork of shrubs or small trees, 3–12 feet high
Size: Inside diameter 2 inches; inside depth 1½ inches
Materials: Fibers from old milkweed stems, fine bark strips, fine grasses, and downy material, such as from willow seeds or the stems of cinnamon fern, and silk from caterpillar nests

Generally the female does all of the building of the nest, although in a few cases males have been observed to participate to a very minor degree. More typically, the male remains in the area of the nest, singing or following the female on her trips to gather nesting material. The female is conspicuous at this time because she builds actively for at least two days, making repeated trips to spots near the nest where she gathers material. The material is often downy or whitish and easily seen as she flies with it back to the nest site. You may see her collecting silk from a tent caterpillar nest. Although most of the nest is completed in about two days, minor additions may continue to be made for a day or two after that. During nest-building, Chip-calls are used by the pair.

Yellow Warblers are frequently parasitized by Brown-headed Cowbirds; one study found as many as four out of every ten nests affected. A common response of the Warblers to finding a Cowbird egg in their nest is to build a new nest right on top of the one with the Cowbird egg in it.

Breeding

Eggs: 4–6, average 5. Whitish with brown-gray blotches concentrated at larger end
Incubation: 10 days average, by the female only
Nestling phase: 9–11 days
Fledgling phase: About 2 weeks
Broods: 1

Egg-Laying and Incubation

There may be a period of a few days after the completion of the nest before the first egg is laid. Generally, one egg is laid each day until the clutch is complete. Incubation starts on or before the laying of the last egg. During incubation, the female may leave the nest to feed on her own or the male may feed her, on or near the nest. In some cases, mate-feeding is done so quickly that it is easily missed. It occurs about once per hour and continues through the incubation period. When not feeding the female, the male generally stays near the nest, feeding and singing.

Nestling Phase

Singing decreases at the time the eggs hatch, possibly just as a result of the male having to gather food for the young. At this time, if the birds are disturbed, the parents may give the Metallic-chip or do a distraction display in which they flutter their wings and fly close to the ground. The area around the nest is defended vigorously during incubation and only slightly less so in the nestling phase.

Both the male and the female feed the young. For the first three or four days, the female broods the young on the nest most of the time. The male brings food to the nest and gives it to her, and she gives it to the young. Sometimes the male feeds the young directly, if the female is off the nest. Right after feeding the young, he may even sing while perched on the nest. After the young are four days old, the female no longer broods them except in cases of rain or too much sun.

In general, the parents eat the fecal sacs for the first few days, then increasingly more often they carry them off. Throughout the nestling phase, both parents tend to come and go from the nest on fixed, separate routes.

Fledgling Phase

After first leaving the nest, the young perch within a foot or two of it. Within the next day they move slightly farther away and are fed there by the parents for the next three days or so. After that, the young are more dispersed but remain within the general boundaries of the territory.

Plumage

DISTINGUISHING THE SEXES In the breeding season the male can be recognized by the prominent reddish streaks that line his breast. The female is recognized by her clear yellow breast, with no streaks or only faint ones at either side. With regard to behavior, only the male gives Song and only the female builds the nest and incubates and broods the young.

DISTINGUISHING JUVENALS FROM ADULTS Juvenals are distinguished from adults by the olive-brown color on their back and their lack of breast streaking.

MOLTS Yellow Warblers undergo two molts per year. There is a complete molt in late summer (July–August) and a partial molt in spring involving all but the tail and wing feathers.

Seasonal Movement

Yellow Warblers migrate almost as soon as they are finished breeding. In many cases they start moving in early July and are gone by August. They are one of the earliest arrivals on the wintering grounds of Central and South America, reaching Guatemala by early August. They travel in large flocks and are a common sight in the South during midsummer. Nine months of the year are spent on their wintering grounds, where males sing and form territories as soon as they arrive. They also give the Chip-call as they defend their areas.

The migration north starts in April and is finished by about mid-May.

Eastern Meadowlark / *Sturnella magna*

THE AUDITORY DISPLAYS OF THE MEADOWLARK ARE FAIRLY EASY TO distinguish and they are one of your best clues to the breeding behavior of these birds. The lovely slurred whistles of the male's Song carry well across the green spring meadows where the birds form their territories. Males arrive before females, sing from exposed perches, chase one another, and do a display called Jump-flight, where they flutter several feet up with their legs down and wings held high. One male tends to do this right after another when the two are involved in a territorial dispute. Other visual displays take place on the ground and may be hard to see among the tall meadow grasses.

Hearing Song from one bird, immediately followed by the Chatter-call from another, usually means that the birds are a paired male and female. The pair tend to stay close together especially just before nest-building begins. Courtship behavior involves chases and Jump-flight as well, so that it is not always easy to distinguish from territorial behavior. The fact that the male and female are identical in plumage may add to the confusion.

Male Meadowlarks are usually polygamous and have two or three females breeding on their territory. If you watch the movements of the females closely, you will soon discover the placement of the nests. This is especially true during the nest-building and nestling phases, when they are making repeated trips to and from the nest. The nest is on the ground and very well hidden, having a dome of grasses woven together above it. It is a beautiful sight, and once you have found it you will have great views of the young as they develop.

BEHAVIOR CALENDAR

	TERRITORY	COURTSHIP	NEST-BUILDING	BREEDING	PLUMAGE	SEASONAL MOVEMENT	FLOCK BEHAVIOR
JANUARY							▓
FEBRUARY						▓	
MARCH	▓	▓				▓	
APRIL	▓	▓	▓	▓		▓	
MAY	▓	▓	▓	▓			
JUNE	▓	▓	▓	▓			
JULY	▓	▓		▓			
AUGUST	▓			▓	▓		▓
SEPTEMBER					▓	▓	▓
OCTOBER						▓	▓
NOVEMBER							▓
DECEMBER							▓

DISPLAY GUIDE

Visual Displays

Bill-Tilt

Male or Female   *Sp Su F*

The bill is pointed up and the body feathers are sleeked.

CALL None

CONTEXT Given during aggressive encounters, may be accompanied by Tail/wing-flash. *See* Territory

Tail/Wing-Flash

Male   *Sp Su F*

Bird rapidly and repeatedly spreads and folds wings and tail. When the tail is spread, its outer feathers flash white.

CALL Dzert-call

CONTEXT Given during aggressive encounters, may accompany Bill-tilt. *See* Territory

Jump-Flight

Male or Female   *Sp Su*

Bird jumps into the air, fluttering four to ten feet up and flying several yards before landing. Wings are fluttered rapidly and are more vertical than in normal flight; tail is raised and feet hang down.

CALL None

CONTEXT When given between two territorial males, one bird does it right after the other; when given between mates, usually just one bird does it without the other imitating it. *See* Territory, Courtship

Fluff-Out

Male or Female   *Sp Su*

Bird fluffs out body feathers and spreads tail, exposing its white edges.

CALL None

CONTEXT Given by males during territorial encounters and by mates during courtship. *See* Territory, Courtship

Auditory Displays

Song

Male   *Sp Su F W*

A series of two to eight long, high-pitched whistles. Several of the whistles may be slurred together. The Song is variable.

CONTEXT Given by males, especially during territorial defense and courtship activities, but also may be heard in any month of the year. Most frequently heard during the beginning of the breeding season prior to incubation. *See* Territory, Courtship

Dzert-Call

Male or Female   *Sp Su F W*

dzert or *dzeeert* A short, strong call irregularly repeated. May precede Chatter-call.

CONTEXT Given when the birds are disturbed and may accompany several visual displays used during territory formation and courtship. *See* Territory, Courtship

Chatter-Call

Male or Female   *Sp Su*

ch'ch'ch'ch'ch'ch An extended chattering call lasting one or two seconds. May be preceded or followed by Dzert-call.

CONTEXT Most often given during interactions between mates. In courtship the female may give Chatter-call immediately after male gives Song. *See* Courtship

Flight-Song
Male   *Sp*

Several whistled notes followed by a fast, twittering warble. Given while bird is in flight

CONTEXT Although Song can also occur during flight, this display is easily distinguished from it by the addition of the twittering warble. It is not common but is a striking occurrence when observed. Its function is unclear, but it seems to suggest extreme excitement and occurs during territory formation and courtship.

Beeert-Call
Male or Female   *Sp Su*

A drawn-out, resonant note, about twice as long as the Dzert-call. Given singly and not usually in association with other calls

CONTEXT May function as an alarm, but also used during Courtship

beeeert or *bjeeert*

BEHAVIOR DESCRIPTIONS

Territory

Type: Mating, nesting, feeding
Size: 3–15 acres
Main behavior: Song, chases, Jump-flights
Duration of defense: From arrival on the breeding ground in spring until the end of breeding

When males arrive on their breeding territories early in spring, you will hear their lilting song drifting across some newly green field. The male, with his bright yellow breast and bold black V, will be visible from one of his singing perches — some prominent pole, fencepost, or tree. The most intense singing occurs in the two to four weeks prior to female arrival. In areas where the Meadowlark is a permanent resident, Song may be heard in any month of the year, but it is most intense prior to the first breeding.

The main elements of Meadowlark territorial behavior are Song, chases, Jump-flights, and various close-range visual displays. Song is the primary territorial display, and you will see neighboring males sitting on prominent perches exchanging Song back and forth. A migrating male that intrudes on a territory is immediately expelled by the owner through a brief chase. A challenging male will not leave the territory as quickly. The territory owner may land near him, and then the two may do several displays, including Bill-tilt, Fluff-out, and Wing/tail-flick. Following this, the two may engage in a long chase over the territory. The chase may last several minutes but at no time does the following bird ever seem to really try to catch the bird it is chasing. If the conflict continues, the two may land in the grass and do Jump-flights. In territorial conflicts, one male will do a Jump-flight and the other tends to do one right after (see Display Guide). More displaying on the ground may occur between Jump-flights. Actual physical combat is rare, but when it does occur it can be quite serious, and males may dig their claws into each other and grapple on the ground.

The average size of a territory is seven or eight acres, but they can range from three to fifteen acres. Territorial boundaries may fluctuate throughout the season. At the beginning of August, there is a decrease in territorial behavior, and the birds move away to other areas where they feed in small flocks. Males may sing in fall but there is no territorial behavior associated with it.

Courtship

Main behavior: Chases, Song and Chatter-call, Fluff-out, Jump-flight
Duration: From arrival of female until start of incubation

Females arrive on the breeding ground two to four weeks after the males. You cannot distinguish males from females by plumage, and even by behavior it is difficult. Thus the arrival of a female is difficult to determine, and, in fact, the Meadowlark's territorial and courtship behavior have many common elements so that it is often difficult to tell them apart.

One clue to identifying the female is that she acts very differently from an intruding male when she enters a territory. At first she does not display with or flee from the territorial male, but moves quietly about the territory feeding. Pairing seems to occur almost at once and with seemingly little ceremony.

Once paired, the birds remain constantly together and go about the territory feeding and looking for a suitable nest site. During this time, when the male sings, the female may immediately respond with the Chatter-call.

An interesting aspect of Meadowlark breeding is that about 60 to 80 percent of the males are polygamous. Usually males have only two females, rarely three. The females all breed in the male's territory, but their breeding cycles are not usually synchronized, so there is not much interaction between them. When aggression occurs, it consists of Bill-tilt and Tail/wing-flash. Usually the male and the females feed peaceably in their territory.

Other types of behavior that occur between mates are aerial

chases, Jump-flights, and copulation. The aerial chases are indistinguishable from those between territorial males. They are long chases with the birds spaced evenly apart throughout, although occasionally the male will try to catch up with the female and seem to peck her. The chases may go over nearby territories, in which case the male of that territory may join in. Also, if a male has more than one mate, she may join as well.

Jump-flights also occur between mates but differ from territorial Jump-flights in that one bird does not immediately display after the other. Jump-flights between mates often occur near the time when the birds are involved with copulation.

As soon as the birds are paired, the male may begin doing the Fluff-out display near the female. Nearer the time of copulation, the male modifies this display by pointing his bill down, erecting his crest feathers, and "strutting" about the female. If the female is unreceptive, she will rebuff him with her own Fluff-out. If she is receptive, she will crouch down, raise her head and tail, and the male will mount her and they will mate.

Nest-Building

Placement: On ground in grasslands, fields, meadows
Size: Height 7 inches; inside diameter 4 inches
Materials: Dried grasses

The female does all the work on the nest. The nest is built in a small depression of one to two-and-a-half inches, which is sometimes partially created by the female as she pecks at and lifts bits of material out. Building is most active in the early morning and late afternoon. It is common for the female to start nests in several locations at first, bringing material to one and then to another. But soon she will concentrate on one spot. Trips to the nest may be made as often as every five to ten minutes, and within a day or two the base of the nest is formed and a dome of grasses is woven together above it. On an average, it takes four to eight days to complete the nest. During this time, the male and female will be actively involved in copulation and its associated displays. Eggs may be laid before the nest is complete.

When there is more than one female on a territory, they may build nests as close as fifty feet, but the nests are usually farther apart.

Locating the Nest

WHERE TO LOOK In fields and grasslands

WHEN TO LOOK Mid-April through June

BEHAVIORAL CLUES TO NEST LOCATION:

1. Look for birds carrying nesting material.

2. Look for birds making frequent trips to the same area.

3. Listen for the Dzert-call, which will be given frequently by the adults as you get near the nest.

Breeding

Eggs: 3–7, most often 5. White, dotted with brown or lavender
Incubation: 13–15 days, by female only
Nestling phase: 11–12 days
Fledgling phase: 4 weeks
Broods: 1–2

Egg-Laying and Incubation

The eggs are laid one each day until the clutch is complete. Incubation is by the female only and begins the day before the last egg is laid. The female stays on the nest day and night, leaving for just short periods during the day to feed. While on the nest, she frequently gets up and turns the eggs. She may make soft clucking noises in response to the Song of the male, but these can only be heard from very close. Incubation takes thirteen or fourteen days, occasionally fifteen.

Nestling Phase

For the first few days after hatching, the female broods the young. Both male and female feed the young, although in many cases the female does most of the feeding. Fecal sacs are removed during the first few days, but by the third or fourth day the young may back up to the nest entrance and defecate over the edge. By the eighth day, the young are active in the nest and their movements may begin to tear apart the dome and cup. By eleven or twelve days, they leave the nest and at this time can usually fly short distances.

Fledgling Phase

After the young leave the nest, they remain dependent on the parents for another four weeks. Their call is like "tseup, tseup." The female feeds the young more than the male does, unless she is starting a second brood, in which case he takes over the majority of the care. By about the third week, the young begin feeding themselves and some may give the Chatter-call. When they are independent, the male may chase them off the territory.

Plumage

DISTINGUISHING MALE FROM FEMALE There is no way to tell male from female through plumage. The male is the only one to give Song and the female is the only one to build the nest and incubate the eggs.

DISTINGUISHING JUVENALS FROM ADULTS Instead of the black V of the adults, the juvenals have just black spots on their upper breast.

MOLT Meadowlarks have one complete molt per year, in late summer and fall.

Seasonal Movement

Most Meadowlarks form large flocks of twenty to three hundred birds and migrate south for the winter, primarily in September and October. However, it is common to find flocks remaining north through the winter, especially along the coast, where they seem to feed and roost near salt marshes.

Migration north in spring occurs in late March and April. The birds migrate at night and feed during the day.

Flock Behavior

In late summer, after breeding is finished, Meadowlarks gather into flocks, some as large as several hundred birds. Some of these flocks move southward but others remain to winter as a flock. The flocks forage in old fields of corn, stubble, and weeds. At night they roost together, often in the tall grass of marshes. Occasionally they join with grackles to roost.

Brown-Headed Cowbird / *Molothrus ater*

THE BROWN-HEADED COWBIRD IS A FASCINATING STUDY IN BEHAVIOR, for in North America it is our only parasitic species, laying its eggs in other birds' nests. There are many questions that immediately come to mind when thinking about the Cowbird's life. How did it evolve its parasitic habits? Did it ever build nests of its own? How do its young recognize their own species, when they were not raised by them? What keeps the young from becoming attached to their foster parents? Very few of these questions have been answered, and for us this makes the bird all the more intriguing. At first, you might wonder why more birds are not parasites—after all, parasites don't need to build a nest, and once they have laid eggs there is no more to it; but there are hidden costs to being a parasite, mainly that the bird gives up control over its eggs and young. Female Cowbirds lay an average of forty eggs per year, but only two or three mature to adulthood.

Cowbirds are marvelous to watch because the males are constantly displaying. From their arrival on the breeding ground until midsummer, you can almost always see several of them perched together doing Song, Bill-tilt, and Topple-over, the peculiar display that makes them look as if they are falling on their faces. These males are vying for dominance, and with that the opportunity to mate with a female. The females are less conspicuous, for a lot of their time is spent quietly observing other birds and trying to locate their nests.

Cowbirds are often cast in the role of the villains, seeming to ruin the broods of other species. But this is far from the case (*see*

Breeding). If you can overcome whatever feelings of mistrust you may have for the birds, you will discover a fascinating species for behavior-watching. Their behavior challenges many preconceived notions about the lives of birds and will expand your view of the many forms that life can take.

BEHAVIOR CALENDAR

	TERRITORY	COURTSHIP	NEST-BUILDING	BREEDING	PLUMAGE	SEASONAL MOVEMENT	FLOCK BEHAVIOR
JANUARY							■
FEBRUARY						■	■
MARCH	■	■				■	■
APRIL	■	■		■			■
MAY	■	■		■			■
JUNE	■	■		■			■
JULY	■	■		■			■
AUGUST					■		■
SEPTEMBER					■	■	■
OCTOBER						■	■
NOVEMBER						■	■
DECEMBER							■

DISPLAY GUIDE

Visual Displays

Bill-Tilt

Male or Female   *Sp Su F*

Bird lifts head and tilts bill up. Feathers may be sleeked.

CALL None

CONTEXT Given by males or females when competing for dominance with another bird. In males, sometimes followed by Topple-over display. *See* Territory, Courtship

Topple-Over

Male   *Sp Su*

Bird fluffs body feathers, arches neck, spreads tail and wings, and seems to fall forward. Display often ends with a brief bill-wiping.

CALL Song

CONTEXT Given on perches or on the ground. Given by males to females or to other males; may function as courtship to females and as a competitive display to males. *See* Territory, Courtship

Head-Forward

Male or Female   *Sp Su F*

Bird fluffs body feathers, raises wings, thrusts head forward.

CALL None

CONTEXT Occurs during territory defense and during feeding when many birds are present. May be given toward other species as well.

Auditory Displays

Song

Male   *Sp Su*

bublowcomseee Several guttural bubbling sounds followed by a long, squeaky whistle.

CONTEXT Given by males during Topple-over in presence of females or other males. *See* Territory, Courtship

Whistle-Call

Male   *Sp Su*

pseeeseeee A long, squeaky, slightly ascending whistle followed by one or more shorter, slightly lower whistles. Lasts two or three seconds.

CONTEXT Given by males while perched or in flight. A very common call that may function as a contact note

Chatter-Call

Female   *Sp Su F*

ch'ch'ch'ch'ch A rapid series of rather liquid sounds, creating a bubbly chatter

CONTEXT Given by the female in a variety of circumstances, such as aggression. May also function as a contact note. *See* Territory, Courtship

Cluck-Call

Male or Female   *Sp Su F*

A short, single sound

CONTEXT Given in times of alarm or danger and occasionally while feeding

BEHAVIOR DESCRIPTIONS

Territory

Type: Mating, nesting
Size: 10–50 acres
Main behavior: Chases, Bill-tilt, Chatter-call
Duration of defense: Throughout the egg-laying period

The type of territorial behavior used by a Cowbird depends on the habitat in which it lives. In the open farmlands of the Midwest where host species are less numerous and more concentrated at field edges, Cowbirds are not territorial. Instead, small flocks of males remain in fixed areas while females roam more widely in search of suitable nests in which they will lay their eggs.

In mixed deciduous woodlands where host species are numerous and widely dispersed, Cowbirds are territorial. The females return in early spring and form territories of from ten to fifty acres. They compete with other females at the borders of territories, using Bill-tilt, Head-forward, and Chatter-call. They keep other females out of the territory at least during the morning hours. Later in the day, all Cowbirds in a given area feed together at certain prime feeding spots, whether these exist in a bird's territory or not. Males may defend a mate from other males but they do not defend a territory.

Courtship

Main behavior: Topple-over, Bill-tilt, and Song
Duration: March to July

The type of mating system Cowbirds use varies with their territorial behavior (*see* Territory). In Midwest farmlands where the birds are not territorial, they have a promiscuous mating system. The males remain in small, loose flocks that stay in areas of twenty to one hundred acres. A common sight in one of these flocks is the males, either perched or on the ground, displaying to each other, using the Topple-over, Bill-tilt, and Song. Through these displays, males are competing for dominance in that area. Females roam widely in search of nest sites. When they are ready to mate and lay eggs, they mate with the dominant male in an area. Thus, each female may mate with a number of males.

In deciduous woodland areas of the East, the females have fixed territories but males do slightly more roaming. Here they have a monogamous mating system. Males compete with each other for dominance in a female's territory using Topple-over, Bill-tilt, and Song. The dominant male then "guards" the female by following her wherever she goes in her territory. When other males come near, he gets between his mate and the other male and does Topple-over, Bill-tilt, and Song, which usually makes the other male leave. The male may do Topple-over toward the female, in which case she may either mate with him or give the Chatter-call and Head-forward displays, rebuffing his attempt. The dominant male guards the female, for she will mate with whatever male she is near. Courtship behavior continues through the egg-laying phase, which stops about midsummer.

The male and female may use the Chatter-call and Whistle-call as contact notes as they take flight and land. Generally, in the early morning the female spends time looking for host nests, and she seems to prefer doing this alone. If a male follows her at this time, she will be aggressive toward him.

Nest-Building

Female Cowbirds lay their eggs in the nests of other birds, so their problem is not building but finding nests. Cowbirds have been found using the nests of over one hundred fifty species, but by far the most commonly used species are among the Warblers, Vireos, Flycatchers, and Finches. A list of some of the most common hosts is at the end of this section.

Nest-searching takes place primarily in the morning, and the female usually does it alone. Females have several methods for

*Cowbird egg in
Yellow Warbler
nest*

locating nests. One frequently used is to perch fairly high up in trees and quietly watch the activities of birds around her.

Another method is for the female to move about in scrubby or forested areas where birds are actively building. In this case the female may be walking along the ground or moving low among shrubbery. In a third method, the female repeatedly flies into shrubbery, making noises and flapping a great deal. This tactic may be designed to scare up the nesting birds and make apparent the location of their nest.

From a behavior-watcher's point of view, the female Cowbird is obviously a sharp observer, for she must continually locate the whereabouts of new nests as she lays eggs throughout the season.

BEHAVIORAL CLUES TO LOCATING THE NEST Locating a Cowbird egg depends on your watching the movements of the female and on locating the nests of other species. Below is a list of the most commonly parasitized species. Many of them are discussed in either volume 1 or volume 2 of *A Guide to Bird Behavior,* and you can look in the Nest-building section for these species to help you locate their nests.

Eastern Phoebe, vol. 2	Yellow-breasted Chat
Wood Thrush, vol. 2	American Redstart
Veery	Red-winged Blackbird, vol. 1
Red-eyed Vireo, vol. 1	Northern Cardinal, vol. 2
Warbling Vireo	Indigo Bunting, vol. 2
Yellow Warbler, vol. 2	Rufous-sided Towhee, vol. 2
Ovenbird	Chipping Sparrow, vol. 2
Common Yellowthroat, vol. 1	Song Sparrow, vol. 1

It should be mentioned that, even with this large number of eggs laid, the Cowbird population is not growing any faster than that of other species. This is because only a small proportion of the eggs laid by a female Cowbird live to be adults due to predation and host defenses.

Cowbirds usually lay eggs after the host has started laying, although occasionally they lay their egg first in a nest. Eggs are laid early in the morning at a time when the host is not near the nest. Occasionally the female Cowbird will remove one of the host eggs, often eating it and carrying away the shell before she lays her own. In areas where females do not have territories (*see* Territory) or where territories overlap, more than one Cowbird may lay an egg in a single nest.

There are several responses of the host to Cowbird eggs. One is to recognize the foreign egg, puncture it, and remove it. This is typical of Robins and Catbirds. Several other species have a tendency to desert the nest or build another nest on top of their present nest when they find a Cowbird egg. This is true of the Yellow Warbler and Phoebe. Other birds seem to accept the Cowbird egg and incubate it as if it were their own. This is true for most of the species listed as common hosts in the previous section.

Breeding

Eggs: Usually 1 per host nest. Off-white with brownish spots
Incubation: 10–13 days
Nestling phase: 9–11 days
Fledgling phase: Not known

Egg-Laying and Incubation

Once a Cowbird lays its eggs in another bird's nest, its parental duties are done, for the other bird incubates and raises the young. A female Cowbird lays an average of forty eggs per breeding season. Usually she does not lay more than one egg in a nest, possibly because the young would then compete with each other. Females seem to lay eggs in groups of about five or six eggs, usually one each day, and then they have a period of a few days when they do not lay.

Incubation for Cowbird eggs ranges from ten to thirteen days. The variation may stem from the incubation habits of the host. Usually the Cowbird egg hatches slightly before those of the host, giving the nestling a head start on feeding and growing.

Nestling Phase

Two features of Cowbird development help make them successful nest parasites. Their incubation period is generally shorter than that of their hosts, and their growth rate for the first few days of nestling life is very rapid. Because of these factors, the nestling Cowbird is usually much larger than the young of the host, gets the greater share of the food, and in some cases actually crowds the other young out of the nest.

It is commonly believed that when there is a Cowbird in a nest, none of the brood of the host survive. Careful studies of parasitized nests indicate otherwise. Nests in which Cowbirds are successfully raised typically also produce successful fledglings of the host as well. In one study it was shown that a successfully raised Cowbird reduces the brood of the host by only one fledgling.

The length of the nestling phase for the Cowbird depends on the ability of the host parents to feed it. In any case, the Cowbird usually leaves the nest before the young of the host.

Fledgling Phase

This is the stage when you're most likely to see young Cowbirds, for your attention is attracted to the sight of some smaller species feeding a huge fledgling. The call of the fledgling Cowbird is a distinctive buzzy note continually repeated. The length of the fledgling period is not known.

Plumage

DISTINGUISHING THE SEXES The sexes are easily distinguished, since the male is black with a brown head and the female is all gray-brown.

DISTINGUISHING JUVENALS FROM ADULTS Juvenals are similar to the female in color but are lighter and slightly streaked underneath.

MOLTS Adults have one complete molt per year, in late summer and early fall.

Seasonal Movement

Cowbirds migrate in large groups in spring and fall, usually in the company of Red-winged Blackbirds, Rusty Blackbirds, and Common Grackles. Fall migration continues from September through November, with the majority of birds moving in October. The birds winter in the southern states and Central America, though some may remain quite far north along the coasts.

Spring migration starts early in March, with the birds reaching their breeding grounds in early April.

Flock Behavior

Through most of the year, Cowbirds spend each night in large communal roosts. In summer these roosts may contain just Cowbirds but in the rest of the year they contain other species as well, such as Red-winged Blackbirds, Common Grackles, House Sparrows, and Starlings. On their wintering grounds in the South, there are roosts of almost a million birds, 400,000 of which are Cowbirds. On their first arrival in spring, the birds may continue to roost at night with Red-winged Blackbirds.

Feeder Behavior

Cowbirds are great feeder birds to observe because they are readily attracted by food, are used to feeding in groups, and perform their courtship and dominance displays constantly during their breeding season. See the Display Guide and sections on Territory and Courtship.

MOST COMMON DISPLAYS Look for Bill-tilt among birds feeding on the ground — they are not watching the sky, this is a display. Males do Topple-over and give Song to females and other males. Head-forward may be given during aggression while feeding.

OTHER BEHAVIOR These birds feed communally — that's why you may see more than one female and many males. You may hear the Whistle-call of the male, the Chatter-call of the female. In times of danger the birds give the Cluck-call.

Northern Oriole / *Icterus galbula*

FROM THE MOMENT THEY ARRIVE ON THE BREEDING GROUND, NORTH-ern Orioles are a colorful and active addition to our bird popula-tion. It seems as if every street with tall trees has a pair of Orioles weaving their nest from the tips of drooping branches, chattering and whistling their Song. You would think that with all of their color and volume their behavior would be well known, but amaz-ingly enough, of all the birds in this book, they are perhaps the least studied. Much more close observation needs to be made of their behavior and visual and auditory displays.

The Northern Oriole is another bird — like the Cardinal, Wood Thrush, Scarlet Tanager, and Rose-breasted Grosbeak — in which both the male and female give Song. The males arrive first on the breeding ground and sing from prominent perches in their terri-tory. Neighboring males often engage in countersinging and some-times this takes on the quality of one bird imitating the calls of the other. Intruders are aggressively chased out, and interactions with Wing-droop and the Chatter-call may also occur.

When the females arrive, males may chase them at first, but this gradually gives way to other displays, such as Bowing and Song-flight. Once paired, males and females stay in fairly continuous aural contact, using short Song phrases, Chatter-call, and Weeet-call.

The marvelous suspended nest of the Northern Oriole is perhaps its best-known feature. It is built by the female soon after her arrival and is woven of fibers she pulls from plant stalks, especially from old milkweed stalks. The nest, built at the tip of a branch, sways a great deal in the wind but is extremely strong and often remains on the tree through the winter. In fall, when the nests become obvious on the leafless trees, it is often amazing to see how many pairs of Orioles nested in areas you passed by all summer.

BEHAVIOR CALENDAR

	TERRITORY	COURTSHIP	NEST-BUILDING	BREEDING	PLUMAGE	SEASONAL MOVEMENT	FLOCK BEHAVIOR
JANUARY							
FEBRUARY							
MARCH							
APRIL						■	
MAY	■	■	■				
JUNE	■	■	■	■			
JULY	■			■			
AUGUST					■	■	
SEPTEMBER					■	■	
OCTOBER							
NOVEMBER							
DECEMBER							

DISPLAY GUIDE

Visual Displays

Bowing
Male   *Sp Su*

Bird repeatedly bows forward, lowering head and exposing orange back. Tail and/or wings may be slightly spread.

CALL Melodic version of Song

CONTEXT Done by male in front of female he is courting. *See* Courtship

Wing-Droop
Male or Female   *Sp Su F*

Wings are drooped well below the level of the tail and the tail may be raised up.

CALL Chatter-call or none

CONTEXT Used during aggressive interactions and sometimes by female to her mate during early courtship. *See* Territory, Courtship

Song-Flight
Male   *Sp Su*

Bird flies with slow stalling flight, with wings and tail fanned.

CALL Melodic version of Song

CONTEXT Occurs during courtship and territorial interactions. May be given by the male in view of the female. *See* Territory, Courtship

Auditory Displays

Song

Male or Female   *Sp Su*

A series of about four to eight whistled notes given in succession. Some notes may repeat a given pitch and some may be slightly slurred. Occasionally the notes may be more melodic, like the Song of a Robin.

CONTEXT Given between males in territory formation and between males and females during courtship. Especially in the former, countersinging may occur, with Songs of the two birds being very similar. The melodic version is usually given by the male and accompanies visual displays. *See* Territory, Courtship

Chatter-Call

Male or Female   *Sp Su*

ch'ch'ch'ch'ch   A rapid series of harsh notes, creating a chatter

CONTEXT Given by birds in aggressive interactions and by members of a pair as they approach the nest. Also given in times of alarm. *See* Territory, Courtship, Breeding

Weeet-Call

Male or Female   *Sp Su*

A single, upward-slurred whistle. Short and sometimes soft

CONTEXT Given by the birds when coordinating activities near the nest. May be a kind of contact call. *See* Breeding

Alarm-Call

Male or Female   *Sp Su*

Two clear, unslurred notes in succession, the   *teeetooo teeetooo*
first often higher than the second

CONTEXT Given near the nest at times of imminent danger, especially in response to Crows or other predators near the nest. *See* Breeding

Fledgling Calls

Male or Female   *Su*

When being actively fed, they give a rapid series of "seeseeseesee" notes, usually either ascending or descending. When not being actively fed, they may give a soft "peep" reminiscent of shorebird calls.

BEHAVIOR DESCRIPTIONS

Territory

Type: Mating, nesting, feeding
Size: A few acres
Main behavior: Song, chases, Chatter-call
Duration of defense: From arrival of male to end of breeding

Male Orioles arrive on their breeding grounds in late spring and begin setting up territories, frequently in the same place they bred the year before. They are conspicuous because of their memorable, clear whistled notes and their brilliant orange, black, and white plumage.

Territories are small, often only a few acres, and often adjacent to those of other Northern Orioles. Males give Song from prominent perches within their territory, and frequently engage in countersinging with neighboring males. In some cases, it seems as if one male is imitating the Songs of the other. In a given geographical area, the Orioles may have quite similar versions of Song, while in other areas the Songs may be quite different. Intruding birds are usually chased out, and these chases may be accompanied by Chatter-calls. During pauses in the chases, one or both birds may do Wing-droop. Song-flight, where the bird flies slowly, giving Song, with wings and tail spread, may be a form of territorial advertisement, but this is not known for sure.

Once females arrive, they also participate in territorial defense, chasing other females out of the area.

Courtship

Main behavior: Chases, Bowing, Chatter-call, Wing-droop
Duration: From arrival of female until incubation phase

Courtship starts as soon as the female arrives on the male's territory. At first the male may repeatedly chase after the female, sometimes even displacing her from a perch. Then while the two are perched near each other, the male hops excitedly from perch to perch near the female, while she may give the Chatter-call and Wing-droop. She may then fly off and the male follow her again.

Later in courtship you may see the male do Bowing, where he lands in front of the female, bows low, jerks up, and then bows low again. This may be repeated several times and the wings and tail of the male may be spread. He may also give a melodic version of Song during the visual displaying.

Song-flight, where the male flies slowly with wings and tail spread while giving Song, may also function in courtship.

Nest-Building

Placement: 6–60 feet off the ground, usually at the outermost end of a branch
Size: 3½–8 inches in length
Materials: Strips of plant fibers, string, horsehair, grape bark, grasses, spanish moss

Orioles are as well known for their nests as they are for any other aspect of their behavior. The nest is a long woven sack, suspended from the tip of a drooping branch. These nests are obvious in winter, especially hanging over roads, and it's always interesting to see how many Orioles actually nested in your area, even though you were unaware of them during their breeding season.

Usually just the female builds the nest. First a few long fibers are attached to the branch and looped underneath. After that, she brings other fibers one at a time and pushes them through one side, and then arbitrarily pulls fibers in from the other side. The actions are random and not indicative of any advanced weaving skills, but even so, she gradually creates a suspended mass of material. Then, entering from near the top, she lines it with soft material such as feathers, grasses, wool, and dandelion or willow fuzz. The nest can take from five to eight or more days to complete. Orioles usually build a new nest each year, but in some instances they have been known to repair old nests. When building a new nest, they frequently take material from one of their old nests or some other bird's nest.

While the female is building, the male remains nearby and will sing and give the Chatter-call. He may sometimes go to the nest and poke at the material. The female also gives bits of Song and Chatter-call while she is building.

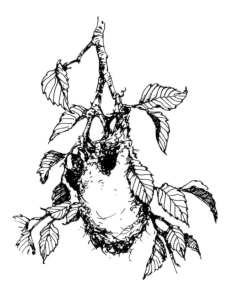

Locating the Nest

WHERE TO LOOK In tall trees, particularly ones with drooping branches, along roadsides or wood margins

WHEN TO LOOK In spring as soon as the birds arrive

BEHAVIORAL CLUES TO NEST LOCATION:

1. Watch for female gathering nest material, such as plant fibers. Or put out some nest material yourself, such as white or neutral-colored string, and see if she takes it.

2. Find an Oriole territory by listening and looking for the birds; their colors are conspicuous and they are continuously noisy during the breeding season, singing and giving Chatter-call.

Breeding

Eggs: 4–6. Pale bluish- or grayish-white with irregular brown blotches
Incubation: 12–14 days, by female only
Nestling phase: 12–14 days
Fledgling phase: 1 week or more
Broods: 1

Egg-Laying and Incubation

The eggs are laid one per day, and the female does all of the incubating. During this time the male moves around the territory singing, and giving Chatter-call if he senses any danger. The female may respond to him with Song or Weeet-calls from the nest. Whenever the female leaves or arrives at the nest, she will give either Chatter-call or Weeet-call. At this stage, hearing these calls is often a good way to locate the nest.

Nestling Phase

The young remain in the nest twelve to fourteen days, and during this time they are fed by both parents. When the nestlings are about one week old, they begin to give calls from the nest. The calls become louder as the young get older. When they are ready to leave the nest, they may at first cling to the outside and then climb in and out.

As in the incubation phase, the parents are quite vocal near the nest. Song fragments are given from near the nest by male and female, and either bird also gives Chatter-calls or Weeet-calls while entering and leaving the nest.

Fecal sacs are carried away from the nest by either parent.

Fledgling Phase

Young Orioles are as incessantly noisy outside the nest as they were in it. They follow the parents around, begging noisily, and are fed for a week or more. The calls of the fledglings may be somewhat variable, but they are always conspicuous. See Display Guide.

The adult female may leave her fledglings a few days before the male and start molting. During this time she roams widely. The young are cared for by the male for another one to two weeks, at which time they are independent. Then they leave the breeding ground and start to migrate south. The adult males remain on their breeding territories through their molt and then depart in late summer.

Plumage

DISTINGUISHING THE SEXES Male is deep orange with black upper back, wings, and head. Female is yellow-orange with olive-brown upper back, wings, and possibly head. Females have two wingbars, males have one. Males in first year are still brownish on head and wings and may be difficult to tell from older females.

DISTINGUISHING JUVENALS FROM ADULTS Juvenals are difficult to distinguish from adult females, but they are often very pale on the belly and have buff wingbars.

MOLTS Adults undergo one complete molt per year, in August and September, or earlier for the female. Young birds have an additional molt in the spring of their first year. In the fall of their first year they follow the schedule of the adults.

Seasonal Movement

In August, females and juvenals may start drifting south while undergoing their molt. Males tend to remain on their territories to complete their molt and then leave. Fall migration occurs in August and September.

Most birds winter in Central America and in northern South America. There they glean insects from leaves, and they also feed on flower nectar. Some evidence suggests that male Orioles may defend feeding territories on their wintering grounds.

In recent years, greater numbers of Northern Orioles have wintered in North America, particularly along the Atlantic coast. These birds are almost always found at bird feeders, where they eat oranges and fruit, peanut butter and cornmeal-fat mixtures. They are especially attracted to areas with many broad-leafed evergreen shrubs and trees.

The birds start their spring migration in April, and most have arrived on their breeding ground by mid to late May. The males seem to arrive a few days ahead of the females.

Scarlet Tanager / *Piranga olivacea*

AS WITH MANY OTHER BIRDS THAT LIVE IN THE FOREST CANOPY, Scarlet Tanagers are far more common than is generally believed. Listening to their auditory displays is the best way to realize the prevalence of the bird. The male sings a great deal, and the extremely common Chip-burr-call is given by either sex when there is any disturbance. These auditory displays will help you locate the birds. The male's contrasting bright-red body and black wings and tail are easy to spot; the female is harder to see, for she is exactly the same color as the sunlit leaves within which she feeds and nests.

During courtship and nest-building the pair usually stay fairly close together, and because of this, the bright colors of the male may help you locate the female. She is most easily seen during the mornings when nest-building occurs, flying down to the ground to collect grasses, twigs, and rootlets. She does not seem to be bothered by observers as she tries to pull up grasses or break off twigs. During nest-building you also have a good chance of seeing copulation, which is repeated often in this species and occurs on prominent perches. The female may interrupt any of her activities to initiate mating by crouching down, Wing-fluttering, and giving a soft, high, repeated call.

The fledglings are easily distinguished from the adults, for they have none of their bright colors; rather, they are brown with slight streaking. In late summer the adults have a complete molt, and for a while, as in spring when they molt again, the male is a mixture of the red summer plumage and yellow winter plumage. In late summer when the molt is complete, he looks just like the female but can be distinguished by his black rather than brown wings and tail.

BEHAVIOR CALENDAR

	TERRITORY	COURTSHIP	NEST-BUILDING	BREEDING	PLUMAGE	SEASONAL MOVEMENT	FLOCK BEHAVIOR
JANUARY							
FEBRUARY							
MARCH					▓		
APRIL	▓				▓	▓	
MAY	▓	▓	▓			▓	
JUNE	▓	▓		▓			
JULY	▓			▓			
AUGUST					▓		
SEPTEMBER					▓	▓	
OCTOBER					▓	▓	
NOVEMBER							
DECEMBER							

DISPLAY GUIDE

Visual Displays

Wing-Flutter
Female   *Sp Su*

The bird crouches, raises bill, and flutters wings close to body.

CALL A soft, repeated sound

CONTEXT Used by the female when she is initiating copulation and when she is receiving food from the male during mate-feeding. *See* Courtship

Wing-Droop-Tail-Up
Male or Female   *Sp Su*

Bird droops wings, revealing red back, and raises the tail. Tail is flicked with accompanying call.

CALL Chip-call or Chip-burr-call

CONTEXT Given by males during territorial encounters and by males and females during aggressive encounters or in presence of danger. *See* Territory

Wing-Droop
Male   *Sp Su*

Bird droops wings and moves about close to ground. Distinguished from Wing-droop-tail-up by lowered tail, lack of call, and context

CALL None

CONTEXT Given by male near the ground usually as the female follows ten to twenty feet above him. *See* Courtship

Auditory Displays

Song

Male or Female   *Sp Su*

jeeyeet jeeeay
jeeeoo jeeyeer

A series of five to nine slightly buzzy whistles; likened to a Robin with a "hoarse voice"

CONTEXT Given by the male throughout the breeding period and occasionally by the female. *See* Territory, Courtship

Chip-Burr-Call

Male or Female   *Sp Su F*

chip'burrr
chip'burrr

A short, two-part call

CONTEXT Given when there is any disturbance, and at other times, such as early in the morning or late in the evening, when no disturbance is evident; sometimes given along with Song fragments

Chip-Call

Male or Female   *Sp Su F*

A single harsh "chip"

CONTEXT Given by male or female at times of alarm or imminent danger. A flicking of the tail may accompany the call.

Sweee-Call

Male or Female   *Sp Su*

A long, high-pitched note, rising slightly at the end

CONTEXT Given softly by either member of the pair, especially when they are close together, early in the breeding cycle. *See* Courtship

Tseah-Call

Male or Female   *Sp Su*

A short, slightly harsh whistle, descending in pitch at the end

CONTEXT Given by birds near the nest, possibly as a signal during nest exchange

BEHAVIOR DESCRIPTIONS

Territory

Type: Nesting, mating, feeding
Size: 2–6 acres
Main behavior: Song, chases, Chip-call, Chip-burr-call, Wing-droop-tail-up
Duration of defense: From arrival on breeding ground through nestling phase

Male Scarlet Tanagers arrive a few days before the females and immediately begin restricting their activities to an area of a few acres. They sing almost continuously through the day, using the highest perches on trees except when they periodically move lower to forage. Countersinging frequently occurs between males in adjacent territories.

Disputes over territorial borders usually cause males to sing shorter Songs more rapidly and to intersperse the Songs with the Chip-call and Chip-burr-call. Visual displays used in these disputes include the Wing-droop-tail-up display, usually given by the more dominant male. Short chases displacing intruders from an area are common.

Courtship

Main behavior: Sweee-call, Song, Wing-droop, copulation, mate-feeding
Duration: From arrival of female into nestling stage

The female Scarlet Tanager arrives a few days after the male. She is often inconspicuous, but one sign of her arrival on a territory is that the male shows a marked reduction in Song and spends less time at his high perches. The male follows the female about as the two forage in the understory shrubs and trees, and the two may exchange Sweee-calls. If the female wanders out of the male's territory, he usually chases her back in.

A fairly inconspicuous display of the male starts to be given around this time. This is Wing-droop, where the male lowers his wings, exposing the red of his back. He does this within a few feet of the ground and always while hopping along in areas where the female is perched above him. Both birds are quiet and the female seems to move along with him ten to twenty feet above.

Copulation may occur after the Wing-droop display, but more often it is initiated by the female, who flies to an exposed horizontal perch, flutters her wings, lifts up her head, and gives a soft, repeated call heard only from close up. The male flies to her and hovers above her back, making contact and mating while he hovers. It lasts only several seconds but then may be quickly repeated. Copulation is done frequently and is commonly seen. It continues into the nestling phase, and you are apt to see it while you are watching other behavior, such as nest-building or feeding young. It usually occurs within forty to fifty feet of the nest.

The male and female Scarlet Tanagers give Song, and the songs are usually indistinguishable, although in many cases female Song is softer and shorter. The female seems to sing most while gathering nesting material or food. At times she may sing almost continuously, and at other times the two may alternate Song. The function of this singing is unclear, although it may help the birds keep in contact during separate activities.

Scarlet Tanagers also do mate-feeding. For many species, mate-feeding occurs early in the breeding season, when it may have more ritual than practical function; but the Scarlet Tanagers do not start until the female is incubating. The female does the Wing-flutter display as in copulation and receives food from the male either at or away from the nest. Mate-feeding stops when the young hatch.

Nest-Building

Placement: On a horizontal limb where small twigs have grown, 5–75 feet above ground, average 20–30 feet
Size: Inside diameter 2½ inches; inside depth 1 inch
Materials: Twigs, grasses, plant stems, rootlets; also bark strips and occasionally string

The female does all of the building of the nest. She flies to the ground to collect grass and other plant stems, often fluttering and tugging to get them loose. Trips to and from the nest may be as frequent as every one or two minutes, and most building is done in the first half of the morning. During nest-building the male either accompanies the female while she is gathering materials or sings from perches in the mid-forest level. Occasionally the female sings while collecting materials, and when flying to and from the nest may give the Sweee-call. The nest takes three to seven days to complete. Any disturbance near the nest will result in one or both birds approaching and giving the Chip-burr-call.

While watching nest-building you may also see copulation: the female interrupts her activities and does Wing-fluttering on a perch near the nest as the male flies over, hovers above her, and mates. The female may then resume building.

Locating the Nest
WHERE TO LOOK In mature deciduous forests
WHEN TO LOOK Late spring and early summer

1. Listen to male or female Song to locate territory.
2. Watch activities of the female, especially in the mornings starting a few days after she arrives.

Breeding

Eggs: Average 4. Pale blue-green with irregular dots of brown
Incubation: 12–14 days by female only
Nestling phase: 9–10 days
Fledgling phase: About 2 weeks
Broods: 1

Egg-Laying and Incubation

Eggs are laid one a day until the clutch is complete, and incubation starts with the laying of the last egg. The female does all of the incubation, frequently changing her position on the nest and periodically standing on the nest rim and turning the eggs over with her bill. She may leave the nest to feed on her own or she may join the male, who will give her food when she does the Wing-flutter display. Sometimes the male comes to the nest either in the absence of the female or to feed her on the nest. In either case, the visits are only seconds long. The rest of the time the male forages about the territory, sings, and chases intruding male Tanagers. The amount that the male feeds the female during incubation varies with different birds from a great deal to none at all.

Nestling Phase

The nestling phase is fairly short for Scarlet Tanagers, being only nine or ten days. For the first three days after hatching, the young are brooded during the day by the female. During this time, the male brings food directly to the young or gives it to the female, who either eats it herself or feeds it to the young. During the nights the female always broods the young. By the fourth or fifth day, you may be able to hear sounds at a distance from the nest, which are given by the young as they are fed. Feeding intervals average about every ten minutes, and the proportion of food each sex brings to the young varies from pair to pair. For the first half of this phase, the fecal sacs are eaten by the parents; after that they are carried away from the nest and dropped.

Fledgling Phase

The young remain in the area of the nest for about two weeks after fledging. They are fed by both parents, and they call noisily a great deal of the time. The somber streaking of the juvenal plumage is in marked contrast to the colors of the adults; so much so that when you first see them being fed by the parents, they seem to be a different species of bird.

Plumage

DISTINGUISHING THE SEXES In summer, male is brilliant scarlet with black wings and tail; female in summer is yellowish beneath, olive-green above, with brown wings and tail. Female in winter is same as in summer. Male in winter is similar to female except for its black wings and tail.

DISTINGUISHING JUVENALS FROM ADULTS Juvenals are distinct from adults, being brown and faintly streaked above, whitish with brown streaks below.

MOLTS Tanagers undergo two molts per year: a complete molt in late summer and fall (July to October), and a partial molt of body feathers in spring. During molts the males show lovely mixtures of red and yellowish feathers.

Seasonal Movement

Fall migration takes place in September and October. The birds migrate either singly or in small groups; either way they are inconspicuous travelers. They are believed to fly south over the Gulf of Mexico and winter in northwestern South America. Movement northward is in April and May, when the birds again travel inconspicuously in small flocks.

Northern Cardinal / *Cardinalis cardinalis*

THE CARDINAL IS A FAVORITE BIRD OF MANY PEOPLE AND IT'S EASY TO see why. The brilliant scarlet plumage of the male and the subtle shades of the female, combined with their clear melodic song, make them enjoyable to watch in any season.

Male and female Cardinals sing equally well, a fact not generally known by those used to the widespread assumption that only male birds sing. Song is an important coordinating behavior in the life of the Cardinal. Cardinal Song consists of many different phrases. In countersinging, one bird will sing one phrase several times and then the other will match it. Then the leader will sing a new phrase and the other will again match it. This type of countersinging that involves copying phrases functions to synchronize and unify members of a pair; and when given between males, helps settle territorial disputes.

At your feeder you may see mate-feeding, a highlight of the relationship between the pair. In this the male picks up a bit of food, hops over to the female, and the two momentarily touch beaks as she takes the food. If you have a pair mate-feeding at your feeder, they are likely to nest in the area. The nest is not hard to find (*see* Nest-Building), and once you know where it is, you will be able to watch mate-feeding continue at the nest through the incubation phase.

BEHAVIOR CALENDAR

	TERRITORY	COURTSHIP	NEST-BUILDING	BREEDING	PLUMAGE	SEASONAL MOVEMENT	FLOCK BEHAVIOR
JANUARY							▓
FEBRUARY	▓	▓					▓
MARCH	▓	▓					
APRIL	▓	▓	▓	▓			
MAY	▓	▓	▓	▓			
JUNE	▓	▓	▓	▓			
JULY	▓	▓	▓	▓			
AUGUST	▓	▓		▓	▓		
SEPTEMBER				▓	▓		
OCTOBER							▓
NOVEMBER							▓
DECEMBER							▓

DISPLAY GUIDE

Visual Displays

Tail-Flick
Male or Female   *Sp Su F W*

Bird quickly flicks tail up and to the side, then more slowly lowers it. Crest is raised.

CALL Chip-call

CONTEXT Given in situations of alarm or possible danger

Head-Forward
Male or Female   *Sp Su F W*

Body is horizontal, bird is slightly crouched, and head is thrust forward. Crest is lowered and bill may be gaped. In intense versions the wings may be fluttered.

CALL None or Chip-call

CONTEXT Given in moments of aggression toward other birds nearby

Song-Flight
Male   *Sp Su*

Bird flies slowly, even momentarily hovering, while using shallow, rapid wingbeats. Crest is up, tail spread, and breast feathers fluffed. Flights may be ten to one hundred feet long.

CALL Song

CONTEXT Male sings as he flies toward female. Occasionally given when no female is evident. *See* Courtship

Lopsided-Pose
Male or Female   *Sp Su*

Bird tilts one side of body up, exposing belly

and creating a lopsided pose. May tilt one side and then the other. Crest is down and wing on raised side of body may be spread. In a variation of this, the bird is more erect with crest raised and sways side to side.

CALLS None or Kwut-call with crest-down version; Song with crest-up version.

CONTEXT Usually given within sight of mate and only a few feet away. Occasionally both may do it together. *See* Courtship

Auditory Displays

Song

Male or Female   Sp Su F W

whoit whoit whoit or wacheer wacheer

A series of clear, whistled notes given in short phrases that are then repeated several times before being varied. Occasionally a soft, churring note follows the Song, but you have to be near the bird to hear it.

CONTEXT Given by males and females in territory formation and courtship. In both situations countersinging may occur, with each bird alternating Song. *See* Territory, Courtship

Chip-Call

Male or Female   Sp Su F W

A short, clean, metallic "chip." May be loud or soft, given singly or in rapid volleys.

CONTEXT A most common call given in a variety of circumstances, including alarm, going to roost, territorial encounters, aggressive encounters, and serving as a con-

tact note between mates. *See* Territory,
Courtship

Kwut-Call

Male or Female   *Sp Su*
A short, harsh call. Not as common as Chip-
call and differs from it in sounding lower, not
metallic, and in being given only singly and
not in volleys.

CONTEXT Given by birds in courtship, aggressive encounters, and during nestling or
fledgling phase when there is possible danger to the young. *See* Courtship, Breeding

Peetoo-Call

Male or Female   *Sp Su*
Two short, unslurred notes, the first often
sounding higher than the second.

CONTEXT Given in aggressive interactions,
sometimes interspersed with Chip-call or
Kwut-call

Fledgling Calls

Male or Female   *Sp Su*
The most common call of the fledglings is
short phrases of rapidly repeated "chip"s.

BEHAVIOR DESCRIPTIONS

Territory

Type: Mating, nesting, feeding
Size: 3–10 acres
Main behavior: Countersinging, chases
Duration of defense: From late winter until the end of breeding

In late winter and early spring, Cardinals that have wintered in flocks begin to disperse into territories and give Song from prominent perches. Birds that did not join a flock but simply spent the winter on their breeding ground just start singing. Males seem to do the majority of active territorial defense and proclamation. A typical behavior is for one male to countersing with a neighboring male, one bird usually following and matching the phrases of the other. This countersinging may be interspersed with chases and Chip-calls.

The countersinging is identical to that between mates in courtship, and we know of no way to distinguish one from the other without locating the participants and seeing what their sex is.

Males or females often intrude on the territories of others, and in these cases, females chase females and males chase males while the other member of the pair plays a fairly passive role. Chases may be interspersed with the birds landing near each other and doing the Head-forward display.

Courtship

Main behavior: Countersinging, mate-feeding, and Lopsided-pose
Duration: From late winter until early summer

If you have a feeder that attracts Cardinals, observe the birds' behavior in late winter, for you may be able to see the first signs of courtship. In winter you may see the male be aggressive to the female while they feed. But at the start of courtship you will see both feeding together peacefully. At this time the male Cardinal may also begin to give some fragments of Song during the day. In the weeks following this, you will see the three main features of Cardinal courtship: countersinging, mate-feeding, and the Lopsided-pose.

Male and female Cardinals sing equally well. Cardinal Song phrases vary from day to day, from bird to bird, and from one region of the country to another. Do not mistake these variations in phrases for different auditory displays; they are still all Song.

In the early stages of courtship, the male and female perch in different areas of the territory and countersing. First one sings a phrase and then the other sings, often matching the same phrase. After a while the first bird may alter its phrase and the other will again match it with its own Song. This countersinging is lovely and may continue for long periods during the day. It is identical to the countersinging of territorial rivals in neighboring territories, so, without actually seeing the birds, you cannot be certain whether you are hearing a pair, two males, or two females.

The next feature of courtship is best seen at your feeder. This is mate-feeding. The male picks up a seed or other food bit, hops over to the female, and tilts his head sideways to place it in her beak. In spring, Cardinal mate-feeding becomes very common and continues into the breeding period in early summer. Mate-feeding can occur as frequently as four times in a single minute.

The third feature of Cardinal courtship is far less commonly observed than the other two. This is the Lopsided-pose, in which one or both birds tilt their body first to one side and then the other, sometimes so quickly that it creates a swaying type of motion. It is most commonly given by the male to the female, and it may be accompanied by Kwut-calls or Song.

In addition to these behaviors, you may see and hear the Song-flight of the male as he flies toward his mate or intruding females. See Display Guide.

Occasionally a lone bird, or member of a neighboring pair, will compete for a bird's mate. These interactions involve chasing of males by males and females by females, much Song, and Chip-calls. The encounters can be quite confusing and may continue over several hours.

Copulation has not been that commonly observed. The female may solicit copulation by crouching with head and tail raised and giving high "see" notes. Sometimes immediately prior to copulation the male, while singing with crest erect, may sidestep or almost slide down a branch to the female. Renewed countersinging between mates may precede a second brood.

Nest-Building

*Placement: In densest part of thicket or low shrub, vine or hedge 2–12
feet high, usually 4–5 feet*
Size: Depth 1⅝ inches; height 3¼ inches; outside diameter 5⅜ inches
Materials: Weeds, twigs, vines, grass, bark, strips of paper, and leaves

Cardinals like to nest in thickets and shrubs, and you can often
find their nests in honeysuckle, privet hedges, multiflora rose, and
dense evergreens. The nest is usually built by the female, and a
common sight is the pair flying across an open space, the female
leading with nesting material in her beak. The male often accompanies her on these gathering trips, but at other times he remains
near the nest, occasionally giving Song. Every time the female
arrives at the nest, she gives several Chip-calls. While gathering
materials, she may break some dry twigs off shrubs or may gather
them from the ground.

There are four layers in Cardinal nests. The first is a platform of
stiff weed stems and vine stems; the second consists of leaves or
paper, and grapevine bark; the third is fine weed stems and grass
and trailing vines; and the fourth is fine rootlets and grass stems.
Occasionally the male may help gather material and even take part
in some building. The nest takes four to six days to complete.

Locating the Nest

WHERE TO LOOK In thickets, dense vines, shrubs

WHEN TO LOOK End of March, from early April on

BEHAVIORAL CLUES TO NEST LOCATION:

1. Look for birds gathering nest material and flying together into thickets.

2. Listen for female singing from the nest. Be alert if male arrives in area with food in his bill; she may meet him or he may fly to her.

Breeding

Eggs: 2–5, usually 3. Grayish or bluish white, spotted or blotched
Incubation: 12–13 days, by female only
Nestling phase: 9–10 days
Fledgling phase: 3–4 weeks
Broods: 1–4

Egg-Laying and Incubation

The eggs are laid one per day until the clutch is complete. The female starts full incubation after the last egg is laid. While the female is incubating, her behavior in relation to the male is variable. Sometimes she gives Song, and this usually makes the male come to the nest and feed her. At other times she may fly to him and combine feeding herself with being fed by him. Sometimes he may sing from around the territory and she will answer from the nest.

Nestling Phase

The female broods the young constantly for the first two days after hatching; after this it is done less and less until by the fifth day she no longer broods. During the first days of the nestling phase, the male brings food for the female and the young. Later both parents gather food for the young. At about seven days after hatching, the young begin to make audible noises from the nest and stretch their heads above the rim. During the last two days of nestling life, the young may be fed as often as eleven times in an hour.

For the first few days, the parents eat the fecal sacs; after that they carry them off.

Fledgling Phase

After first leaving the nest, the young tend to stay perched nearby giving their short volleys of "chip" notes. Both parents bring them food, except in cases where the female is starting another brood and unavailable. As the young gain more flying ability, the family becomes slightly dispersed. If you approach the area where the young are being fed, the parents are likely to give the Kwut-call or Chip-call and fly excitedly about you. If there is an aerial predator in the area, the Cardinals usually give rapid volleys of the Chip-call. If there are multiple broods, the adults may drive off the young when they are independent and it is time to start feeding the next brood.

Plumage

DISTINGUISHING THE SEXES Male and female are easily told apart through plumage. The male is all red and the female is a light brown with reddish overtones.

DISTINGUISHING JUVENALS FROM ADULTS Juvenals are similar to the female but have a black bill rather than a red one.

MOLTS There is one complete molt per year, in late summer and early fall.

Flock Behavior

Cardinals usually gather together in flocks in fall and remain together through winter, staying in areas where food is plentiful. The flock is often fairly evenly divided by sex. They move about together giving Chip-calls and occasionally chasing one another. At night they roost together. The number of birds in a flock remains fairly constant, but individuals may leave and be replaced by others. In these flocks, males may be slightly dominant over females in feeding situations. The flocks break up in late February.

Some Cardinals do not join flocks but remain on their breeding ground with their mate through winter.

Feeder Behavior

A Cardinal pair will be a colorful and welcome addition to the feeder. They will come throughout the year and you can trace the changing nature of their relationship as the breeding season approaches. During the fall and early winter, the male may be mildly aggressive to the female at the feeder. In late winter, the male is more tolerant of her presence. Soon mate-feeding will begin. Sometimes Cardinals gather in flocks in winter and come to feeding areas.

MOST COMMON DISPLAYS Cardinals generally approach the feeder giving the Tail-flick and Chip-call. If they are being aggressive to other birds at the feeder they may do Head-forward.

OTHER BEHAVIOR As part of courtship, you may see the males and females do Lopsided-pose and give Song. The parents frequently bring the young to the feeder, in which case you will hear the fledgling calls and see them being fed.

Rose-Breasted Grosbeak / *Pheucticus ludovicianus*

THE SONG OF THE ROSE-BREASTED GROSBEAK IS GIVEN BY THE MALES AS soon as they arrive on the breeding ground. The male sings from among the leaves at the tops of trees and is not as easy to see as one would expect, given his bright coloring. After the female arrives, Song diminishes and the most common display is the Chink-call, a short, metallic squeak that, once you know it, will alert you to the presence of the birds better than any other means. Later, during the incubation and nestling phases, both male and female use Song and the Chink-call around the area of the nest, and because of this they are quite easy to follow.

One of the loveliest features of the male is the bright red patch on his white breast. The size and shape of this patch varies considerably from male to male, thus enabling you to distinguish and follow the activities of individual males. The females are streaked, brown birds that resemble huge sparrows. In most birds that have such marked sexual dimorphism, there is usually more separation of breeding activities, but in this species both male and female seem to share in incubation and caring for the young, and both birds also give Song.

The nest of the Rose-breasted Grosbeak is an extremely loose structure, and you can often see daylight right up through it from below. It is bulky and composed almost entirely of twigs. Since it is usually built only about ten feet from the ground at the edge of open areas, and the pair give a variety of calls and Song while building, it is often quite easy to find. It is one of the better nests to watch for, since both birds share in the incubation and care of the young, and there is always a lot of coming and going of the adults.

BEHAVIOR CALENDAR

	TERRITORY	COURTSHIP	NEST-BUILDING	BREEDING	PLUMAGE	SEASONAL MOVEMENT	FLOCK BEHAVIOR
JANUARY							
FEBRUARY							
MARCH					▓		
APRIL	▓					▓	
MAY	▓	▓	▓				
JUNE	▓	▓	▓	▓			
JULY	▓			▓			
AUGUST	▓			▓	▓	▓	
SEPTEMBER						▓	
OCTOBER						▓	
NOVEMBER							
DECEMBER							

DISPLAY GUIDE

Visual Displays

Crest-Raise

Male or Female   *Sp Su F W*

Feathers on crest are raised, making the top of the head appear slightly peaked

CALL None

CONTEXT Generally given by the less dominant members of a conflict. *See* Territory

Song-Flight

Male   *Sp Su*

A slow flight with spread tail and shallow wingbeats. White and black patterns of wings conspicuous. Flight may be short or long, straight or circular, rising or level.

CALL Rapid-song

CONTEXT Usually done by the male when leaving or returning to the female during the courtship phase. Wing-droop-fluff may follow. *See* Courtship

Wing-Droop-Fluff

Male   *Sp Su*

At first the bird droops wings, raises tail, and hops in a zigzag pattern along a branch. Then, often at a lower height or on the ground, the bird droops wings and quivers them, spreads and lowers tail, and fluffs lower back and breast feathers. At the same time, the body is slowly rotated from side to side.

CALL Song, often the rapid version

CONTEXT Given near the female during courtship and sometimes prior to copulation. The female may chase the male, in which case both birds may begin to move in high hops. May end in male chasing female. *See* Courtship

Auditory Displays

Song

Male or Female   *Sp Su F*

taweet tawooh
tawhat taweer
A series of loud, slurred whistles. Sometimes described as a Robin in a hurry. There are at least two versions: one with slight pauses between each whistle in the series, and a more rapid one with no pauses.

CONTEXT Song is given in many contexts and quite continuously through the breeding season. Female may sing near the nest or while foraging. Male sings during territory formation, courtship, and when at the nest. *See* Territory, Courtship, Breeding

Chink-Call

Male or Female   *Sp Su F W*
A short, metallic squeak, with a tone similar to squeaky car brakes

CONTEXT Given softly between the pair during close contact and more loudly during moments of alarm or aggression. *See* Territory, Courtship, Nest-building

Eee-Call

Male or Female   *Sp Su*
A prolonged, high-pitched, faint note
CONTEXT Given between the pair near the

nest and during intimate contact. *See* Courtship

Chrr-Call
Female *Sp*
A short, harsh call
CONTEXT Given by the female, possibly dur-
ing her initial courtship encounters with a
male. *See* Courtship

Fledgling Calls
Male or Female *Su*
The young are often quite loud and use a
variety of calls sounding like "tooyou." They
also give the Chink-call. *See* Breeding

BEHAVIOR DESCRIPTIONS

Territory

Type: Mating, nesting, feeding
Size: 2–3 acres
Main behavior: Song, Chink-call, chases
Duration of defense: Throughout breeding season

Male Grosbeaks arrive on their breeding grounds before the
females and start to limit their movements to an area of about two
or three acres. In this area they forage and circulate, giving Song
and the Chink-call. When singing, they may use a vertical posture
in which their wings are slightly drooped, revealing the white
patch on their rump.

In aggressive encounters between neighboring males, the dominant bird usually sings more and chases the intruder out. In many
cases, the intruder may then circle back and reenter the territory; if
he does, he is chased again. During chases the Chink-call or rapid

version of Song may be heard. In close interactions between two males, you may see one of the birds do a flicking of the wings or brief spreading of the tail. These actions usually precede an attack and chase.

If you see more than one male coexisting peacefully in one male's territory, chances are that the others are migrants. Territorial males allow nonsinging migrants to feed in their areas, but if the migrants sing at all, they are driven off.

After females arrive and pair, they may be seen driving other females off the territory. This may be in defense of territory or of mate. *See* Courtship

Courtship

Main behavior: Chases, Wing-droop-fluff, Song-flight
Duration: From arrival of female until egg-laying

The females arrive a few days after the males. For the first few days the female is on a male's territory, the male is likely to be seen chasing her in short, low flights. During these chases you may hear the female give the Churr-call.

A sign that the two are more solidly paired comes in the next three or four days as the two move about the territory; they stay near each other, exchanging Chink-calls and Eee-calls as they forage together. At this time the female may even seem to be slightly dominant over the male, as she occasionally will supplant him from perches and chase him for short distances.

Two other displays occurring during the courtship phase are Song-flight and Wing-droop-fluff. Both of these are given by the male, and the former is the more commonly seen. It can be a spectacular display, especially when the male takes a long flight up into the air, revealing the bold patches of white and black on his wings. At other times Song-flight is shorter and less conspicuous. Following Song-flights, the male and female usually approach each other, and the male may continue displaying with the Wing-droop-fluff. This is an intense courtship display with several variations, all of which include drooping of the wings and fluffing of the rump and breast feathers. Copulation often follows the Wing-droop-fluff. All of these displays continue to be given into the egg-laying phase.

Occasionally pairs in adjoining territories engage in chases and interactions near their borders. Lone females or males that intrude on the territory are chased off by the same-sex resident; the other member of the pair may accompany its mate, but not be directly involved in the chase.

Nest-Building

Placement: 5–25 feet above ground in fork of shrub or tree with dense foliage; vegetation may be deciduous or evergreen
Size: Inside diameter 3½ inches; inside depth 2 inches
Materials: Coarse and fine twigs, often leaves and horsehair

Before nest-building begins, you may see either member of a pair perch in prospective nest sites and then crouch and turn around. This is common for many birds and seems to be a sort of testing of nest sites for suitability. Nests may be started as soon as a week after the female's arrival. How much the pair share in nest-building seems to vary widely. In some cases, only the female goes anywhere near the nest site until the incubation phase. In others, the male assists some in bringing material to the nest. And in at least one case, the male has been observed to sit on the nest and do all construction while the female brought twigs to him.

During nest-building, the male continues to give Song from near the nest site, and both sexes may be heard to give the Chink-call and Eee-call. Occasionally the female may give short versions of Song as well.

The nest is very loosely built and you can often see light through it. It is composed largely of twigs collected from the ground or broken off shrubs and trees. The inner layer is mainly just finer twigs—Hemlock is often a favorite—but may contain some horsehair. The nest takes two or three days to build.

Locating the Nest

WHERE TO LOOK In trees or shrubs at the border of open areas such as fields, roads, or gardens

WHEN TO LOOK In mid- to late spring and again in midsummer when a second brood may be started

BEHAVIORAL CLUES TO NEST LOCATION:

1. Listen for Song from either male or female and locate the bird, for both birds have a tendency to sing from the nest area.

2. Listen for Chink-call or Eee-call and look for either member of the pair carrying twigs.

Breeding

Eggs: 3–6, average 4. Pale blue with irregular brown spots, often more dense at the larger end

Incubation: 12–14 days, by male and female

Nestling phase: 9–12 days

Fledgling phase: 2–3 weeks

Broods: 1–2

Egg-Laying and Incubation

Egg-laying may start even before the nest is finished, and one egg is laid each day until the clutch is complete. Once incubation starts, the eggs are rarely left unattended. Both male and female share in the incubation, the female sometimes doing slightly more than the male. While incubating, the male may give Song and the female may give the Chink-call. When exchanging places on the nest, a shorter and quieter version of Song may be given by either or both birds. The Eee-call may also be heard. If you see the incubating bird stand at the edge of the nest and dip its bill down toward the eggs, it is probably turning the eggs, for this is frequently done by the parents.

Nestling Phase
Once hatched, the young are brooded many times throughout the day for periods of about ten minutes each. Brooding continues through much of this phase, but in the later stages the parent may just stand over the young, possibly to shade them from direct sun. Some observers report having seen only the female brooding. With both parents feeding the young, the nest is rarely left unattended; one bird stays on or near the nest while the other is out foraging. As in the incubation phase, the parents often give a short, soft version of Song when exchanging places at the nest.

When the young are about four days old, you may hear them call as a parent arrives with food. At about six days old, they start calling more constantly, whether a parent is bringing food or not. After feeding, the parents collect fecal sacs. Early in the nestling phase they eat them, but later they carry them off.

If a second brood is started, the female may leave the young of the first brood while they are still nestlings in order to start building her second nest. This second nest may be only thirty feet from the first nest. She may leave the first brood as early as two to six days after hatching, although probably more often she leaves near the end of the nestling phase. When she leaves, the male assumes all care of the young in the first brood.

Fledgling Phase
Soon after the young leave the nest, they are able to fly short distances. They tend to be very noisy, constantly giving calls that

sound like "tooyou." They may move up to a hundred yards from the nest in the first few days and remain in the area, being fed by one or both parents. During the second or third week of the fledgling phase, the parents seem to be more forceful when feeding the young, even jabbing the food down their throats. At times they may peck at the bills of the young after feeding them and even chase them for short distances. These may be signs of the normal breakup of the family and the dispersal of the young.

Plumage

DISTINGUISHING THE SEXES The female is streaked with brown, much like a large version of a sparrow; the male's white belly, red chest, and black head and back make him easy to distinguish from the female during the breeding season.

DISTINGUISHING JUVENALS FROM ADULTS Juvenals are similar to the female adult, except the breast is only slightly streaked on the sides, and the front edge of wing is rosy pink.

MOLTS Rose-breasted Grosbeaks undergo two molts per year: a complete molt in August, and a partial molt in late winter before spring migration. Females look similar in winter and summer, but males in fall change markedly, acquiring plumage with brown and black streaks on their head, neck, and back.

Seasonal Movement

Fall migration occurs mainly in September. At this time the males may have completed enough of their molt that they are less brilliantly colored. The only call heard from males or females is the Chink-call as they move secretively among the treetops. They winter in Central and South America. Spring migration occurs in April and May, and the birds do not usually start singing until they arrive on the breeding ground.

Indigo Bunting / *Passerina cyanea*

THE INDIGO BUNTING HAS AN INTRIGUING MIXTURE OF CONSPICUOUS and hidden behavior. The male, from the time he arrives on the breeding ground, is easily seen and heard as he repeatedly gives his Song from exposed perches at the tops of trees. The female, on the other hand, can be so secretive that you may not know that she has even arrived until she is already in the nestling phase and bringing food to the young.

In many other species where the male is brightly colored, he may help you find the female, as he stays near her. But in the case of the Indigo Bunting, the male and female often lead quite separate lives, so that following the male often gets you no closer to the female.

The nest is usually extremely well hidden, and during incubation the female can slip on and off it for short periods without ever being seen. One feature of the bird's behavior that may help you locate the nest is that if you are anywhere near it, the male and/or female will give the Chip-call, do Tail-flick, and hop about. They may start doing this while you are still thirty to forty feet away. The birds are extremely reluctant to go back to the nest if you are near, but if you retreat a little, wait patiently, and watch the female, she will finally return to the nest.

Once you find the nest, the rest of the bird's life unfolds, and you can watch the parents come and go and see the young develop. If you come to the nest and find it empty before you think the nestlings should have left, don't worry, for the young leave the nest early and are possibly perched quietly in the bushes nearby.

BEHAVIOR CALENDAR

	TERRITORY	COURTSHIP	NEST-BUILDING	BREEDING	PLUMAGE	SEASONAL MOVEMENT	FLOCK BEHAVIOR
JANUARY							
FEBRUARY							
MARCH					■		
APRIL	■				■	■	
MAY	■	■	■	■		■	
JUNE	■	■	■	■			
JULY	■	■		■			
AUGUST	■	■	■	■	■	■	
SEPTEMBER	■			■	■	■	
OCTOBER						■	
NOVEMBER						■	
DECEMBER							

DISPLAY GUIDE

Visual Displays

Tail-Flick
Male or Female   *Sp Su*

The tail is twitched from side to side.

CALL Chip-call

CONTEXT Occurs in times of alarm or danger.

See Breeding

Crest-Raise
Male or Female   *Sp Su*

The feathers on the crest of the head are raised.

CALL Chip-call

CONTEXT A common display occurring during disturbances at the nest or during aggressive encounters with other Indigo Buntings. *See* Territory, Courtship

Moth-Flight
Male   *Sp Su*

With wings fanned, head and tail held up, body feathers fluffed, the bird flies slowly with rapid, shallow wingbeats. Flight may be in an arc, straight, or while drifting down from a height.

CALL Flight-song

CONTEXT Frequently done by territorial males toward the territory of another male. Most frequent in the early morning and at dusk, but may be seen throughout the day. *See* Territory

Body-Fluff

Male or Female   *Sp Su*

The body feathers are fluffed, the wings lifted slightly and vibrated, and the body rotated slowly from side to side.

CALL Song softly given or Chip-call

CONTEXT Between males in aggressive encounters, or by either bird when danger is near the nest. A version of Body-fluff may be done by the female in response to danger during the nestling or fledgling phase, possibly as a distraction display. *See* Territory

Auditory Displays

Song

Male   *Sp Su F*

seeseesoysoy-seerseerseet

A series of paired, high, whistled notes lasting two to six seconds. Each individual has a fixed version of the beginning of its Song, which enables you to identify it through the breeding season. The endings of songs may be varied through the addition or subtraction of several notes.

CONTEXT Given by males from high perches or while feeding. It is used throughout the breeding cycle. *See* Territory

Flight-Song

Male   *Sp Su*

A bubbly, explosive sound, unlike the clear whistles of Song, given while the bird does Moth-flight. Similar to the Long-song of the American Goldfinch.

CONTEXT Given by males during territory formation as the bird does Moth-flight. *See* Territory

Chip-Call

Male or Female   *Sp Su F W*

A sharp "chip" like the hitting of two pebbles against each other. The male's version may be slightly different from the female's, enabling you to distinguish the two by sound alone. Sometimes given in a rapid series

CONTEXT Given in times of alarm, such as your approach near the nest. *See* Courtship, Nest-building, Breeding

Zeep-Call

Male   *Sp Su*

A high, thin, slightly extended call

CONTEXT Given by male, mostly early in breeding season. May have some connection to courtship. *See* Courtship

BEHAVIOR DESCRIPTIONS

Territory

Type: Mating, nesting, feeding
Size: 2–6 acres
Main behavior: Song, chases, Moth-flight
Duration of defense: Throughout the breeding period

Once the males arrive on the breeding ground, they start singing from several high and conspicuous perches within their territory. Singing is most frequent in the early morning and evening, but can be heard throughout the day. When the weather is hot, the birds move down from their early-morning perches to more shaded areas and sing less vigorously. They may also sing a quieter Song less frequently while foraging.

As the season progresses, males often join in singing bouts in full view of each other, and it is likely that they come to recognize each other. You also can come to recognize the different males by their Songs, which consistently have the same phrases (*see* "Song" in Display Guide).

Neighboring males may encroach on each other's territories, in which case they are usually chased out. If an intruder persists, the territory owner may perch near him and do the Body-fluff display. Sometimes new males challenge established territory holders: they fly out toward the other's territory using Moth-flight and its accompanying Flight-song, and then circle back to where they were first perched, sometimes being chased by the other male. This behavior may continue for several days. As territorial encounters become more intense, Song becomes louder and more frequent, and in extreme cases squeaky portions are added to it. It is believed that first-year males frequently challenge adult males and, in so doing, adapt their unformed Song to that of the male they are challenging. They then stop challenging and nest nearby. This may account for the high similarity of phrases in the Songs of males in a given area.

Males generally return to their territories of previous years. Shifts in territory location may occur when a male is unable to attract a mate or just before the start of a second brood.

Courtship

Main behavior: Chases
Duration: A few days

Little is known about courtship in these birds. The female is very inconspicuous and it may even be hard to tell when she arrives. Many observers never see the female until the young are hatched and she is seen bringing food to the nest. It has been noted that some males seem to sing less once they are mated. Also, the male seems to chase the female about persistently for the first few days after she arrives. At this time he may use the Zeep-call, and the female may repel his advances through Crest-raise and the Chip-call.

Nest-Building

Placement: Placed in crotch of shrubs or canes, 2–10 feet off the ground, usually low
Size: Inside diameter 1¾–2¾ inches; inside depth 1½–2½ inches
Materials: Dead leaves, weed stems, grasses, with a lining of finer grasses and possibly hair or downy material. Compact

The female does all of the nest-building and site selection. Nests take three or four days to complete. The male may accompany her to the nest site but does not bring material for construction. Usually he remains high up on his perches, singing. When you get into the area of the nest, the male may approach and give the Chip-call and the female may approach even more closely and "chip." Sometimes these "chips" can begin even when you are still thirty to forty feet from the nest. Nests are placed well within cover, and the birds may come and go from the nest from several directions. This is probably the time the female is most conspicuous, until the nestling or fledgling period.

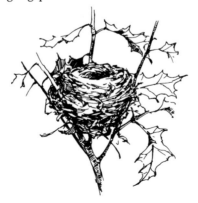

Locating the Nest

WHERE TO LOOK In open, brushy areas, or along the edge of fields or roads

WHEN TO LOOK Late spring and early summer, after female arrives

BEHAVIORAL CLUES TO NEST LOCATION:

1. Look in areas where the male or female give the Chip-call in response to your presence.

2. Follow the female very carefully, especially if she has food in her mouth. Don't get distracted by the male's activity. This is one of the hardest of bird nests to find.

Breeding

Eggs: 3–4. White, unmarked
Incubation: 12 days, by the female only
Nestling phase: 10–12 days, average
Fledgling phase: 2–3 weeks
Broods: 1–2

Egg-Laying and Incubation

During the egg-laying stage, the male stays nearer the female than at any other time in the breeding cycle. This may be for the purpose of mating with her and being sure that no other males do so. The eggs are laid one each day until the clutch is complete. The female does all of the incubation, while the male stays away from the nest, spending most of his time foraging and singing from other areas of the territory.

Nestling Phase

The young hatch over a one- to two-day period. On the first day after hatching, the female broods the young for about 75 percent of the day. Brooding time decreases until the eighth day, when it stops. The female remains on the nest each night.

Some observers say that the male participates in feeding the nestlings; others say he feeds the female away from the nest and she brings the food to the young; but most say that the male does little or no caring for the nestlings and may not approach closer than fifteen feet to the nest. His main activity seems to be guarding the nest from you or other dangers. A good way to know that you are near the nest is to observe the male giving the Chip-call and Tail-flick. The female, especially at the end of the nestling stage, may join him. Watch the female, especially if she has food in her bill. At some point she will become quiet and drop like a stone, straight to the ground, then move along the ground toward the nest and feed the young. It is very hard to follow her. Then she flies up from the nest and continues Chip-calls with the male.

Fledgling Phase
In this stage male and female both feed the young, except in cases where the female starts a second brood; then the male takes over all feeding of first-brood young. When you approach the young, the adult birds use the Chip-call and are very conspicuous. The young stay scattered among the underbrush and give Chip-calls like those of the parents, which probably help the parents locate them. The parents and young of the second brood seem to stay together until they are ready to migrate south.

Plumage

DISTINGUISHING THE SEXES Males are blue; females are all brown. First-year males may have some brown mixed with the blue, and their abdomens may be whitish. The male is the only one to give Song, and the female does all nest-building and incubating.

DISTINGUISHING JUVENALS FROM ADULTS Juvenals look like the female except that their wingbars are buff rather than white.

MOLTS The birds undergo two molts, a complete one in late summer and fall and a partial one in spring. The male looks like the female in winter except for a few blue feathers mixed in with the brown. After the molt in spring, the male's plumage continues to brighten as the gray tips wear off and the bright blue shows underneath.

Seasonal Movement

Indigo Buntings fly south in large flocks from late August into November. They feed during the day in brushy areas abundant with grains and weed seeds. They winter in the same loose flocks in south Florida, Central America, and the northern part of South America.

Migration north takes place in April and May in generally smaller flocks of five to ten birds. Some males may sing some while migrating north. Males seem to precede females, and older males precede younger males. Migration is at night.

Rufous-Sided Towhee / *Pipilo erythrophthalmus*

IF YOU SPEND ANY TIME NEAR TOWHEES, YOU WILL SOON BECOME familiar with two of their auditory displays. The first is the Song of the male, which has often been popularly rendered as "drink your tea," with the last word drawn out and accented. The other is the Chewink-call given by both male and female throughout the season. The common names of the birds, Towhee or Chewink, refer to this call.

Towhees are strikingly colored: the black, white, and rufous color of the male and the white and subtle shades of brown in the female make them beautiful to watch. They are also easy to watch, because they spend so much time either on or fairly close to the ground. Their distinctive way of stirring up the leaves by hopping backward makes them conspicuous during feeding. In fact, listening for this rustling is often a good way to locate the birds.

As soon as the male arrives in spring, he starts continually singing and countersinging with neighboring males. The female arrives soon after, and you can often find her feeding on the ground while the male sings from just above. During their courtship, they do the Tail/wing-spread, which shows off the marvelous black and white patterns of the tail.

Once egg-laying and incubation begin, it is much harder to follow the activities of the birds, for the male rarely comes near the nest until the young hatch, and the female is extremely secretive and very reluctant to return to the nest when there is any sign of danger. The nest is also so well camouflaged that it is hard to find even after you have seen the female arrive and leave several times. But it is well worth the effort of the search, for it is so beautifully blended with the environment of the ground around it. Once you have found the nest, you can return when the female is on it and get amazingly close to her before she flushes.

After the eggs hatch, the male comes to the nest frequently, at first providing the majority of the food for the nestlings and brooding female, and later sharing the work equally with the female.

BEHAVIOR CALENDAR

	TERRITORY	COURTSHIP	NEST-BUILDING	BREEDING	PLUMAGE	SEASONAL MOVEMENT	FLOCK BEHAVIOR
JANUARY							▓
FEBRUARY							▓
MARCH						▓	
APRIL	▓		▓	▓		▓	
MAY	▓	▓	▓				
JUNE	▓	▓	▓	▓			
JULY	▓	▓	▓	▓	▓		
AUGUST	▓	▓		▓	▓		
SEPTEMBER	▓			▓		▓	
OCTOBER						▓	▓
NOVEMBER							▓
DECEMBER							▓

DISPLAY GUIDE

Visual Displays

Wing-Raise
Male   *Sp Su*

The bird briefly raises one wing up in the air and may flutter it. Display may be repeated.

CALL None, or Song given quietly and rapidly

CONTEXT Given during territorial encounters between males. *See* Territory

Tail/Wing-Spread
Male or Female   *Sp*

The tail and/or wings are spread and possibly held open for a few seconds. White spots on tail and wings become prominent.

CALL None

CONTEXT Done between males and females as a part of courtship. A distraction display done during disturbances of the nest may also involve Tail/wing-spread. *See* Courtship, Breeding

Auditory Displays

Song
Male   *Sp Su F W*

A trill about a second long with a predominantly "eee" sound, usually preceded by one or two short preliminary notes. Preliminary notes are most common in eastern subspecies, but are less common or even lacking in western subspecies.

drink your teeeeee or your teeeee or teeeeee

CONTEXT Used by males throughout the year

but mostly in spring and summer. Often given from partially concealed perches or from the ground, while the bird is feeding. *See* Territory, Courtship

Chewink-Call

Male or Female   *Sp Su F W*

The most common call of the Towhee. A short call ranging in sound from "chewink" to the "meow" of a catbird (the latter is more typical of western subspecies)

CONTEXT Given in moments of disturbance or alarm. May also function as a contact call. *See* Territory, Courtship

Quiet-Song

Male or Female   *W Sp Su*

A quiet, extended series of a variety of calls and song parts. A soft, musical warbling. Sung with beak closed.

CONTEXT Usually given when the bird is perched in dense cover or while it is foraging on the ground. May include any of the other calls or song types. This is not a type of "subsong" given by immatures, for it is given by adults throughout breeding season. Function unknown. *See* Courtship

Seee-Call

Male or Female   *Sp Su F W*

A high, thin call, generally soft. May rise or fall in inflection and waver slightly

CONTEXT Often used by the birds while they forage in the underbrush, and may function as a contact call. Only heard from a few feet away

BEHAVIOR DESCRIPTIONS

Territory

Type: Mating, nesting, feeding
Size: ½–2 acres
Main behavior: Song, Chewink-call, Wing-raise
Duration of defense: Throughout the breeding period

After arriving on the breeding ground, migrating males at first remain in small groups for a few days, then disperse to form territories. In areas where the birds are residents, they remain in loose flocks throughout winter, and then disperse in spring. The males form territories by circling around limited areas and frequently singing, either from perches ten to fifteen feet high or from the ground while foraging. When a strange male enters a territory, it is usually just chased off. If the conflict lasts longer, either the owner or intruder may Wing-raise during the encounter, and the birds may also give the Chewink-call or a soft, rapid version of Song.

Once territories are established, there are few conflicts between neighbors, and males usually respond aggressively only to the Songs of strangers. Sometimes there are common feeding areas between territories where all neighboring pairs may feed without conflict. Territories are defended from the beginning of pairing until the end of breeding. Fledgling birds are allowed in any territory and are not bothered except to be chased briefly away from an adult's favored feeding spot.

Courtship

Main behavior: Chases, Tail/wing-spread, Chewink-call
Duration: From arrival of female until egg-laying

Females arrive on the breeding ground a few days after the males begin their territorial behavior. Activities that occur between males and females include chases of a female by one or more males; the Tail/wing-spread by either male or female, showing off the white markings on the feathers; and Quiet-song by the male or female. At this time males may also be seen carrying and then dropping bits of nesting material.

Over the course of a few weeks, the pair become increasingly connected through the mutual answering of the Chewink-call, and they remain in closer contact throughout the day. Often the male sings from the trees above the female while she forages below on the ground. The pair begin to spend the majority of their time within a smaller portion of the territory, and this is usually where they build their nests.

You can come to recognize paired males through changes in their behavior. They decrease the amount of their singing, they move about less frequently, and they utilize a smaller portion of their territory. Unmated males continue to sing a great deal and circulate around the entire area of their territory at regular intervals.

Nest-Building

Placement: Usually on the ground, occasionally up to 6 feet off the ground. Placed under cover of a small shrub, branch, or group of plants
Size: 3¼ inches inside diameter; 2¼ inches inside depth
Materials: Leaves, weed stalks, strips of bark, grasses, lined with fine grasses and sometimes hair

Nests are most often placed in a slight depression, possibly made by the bird, making the top of the nest flush with the ground. Nests are located in fairly exposed areas, such as under a lone shrub, rather than deep within thickets. Usually some type of branch or leaves hang over the nest.

The female does all collecting of material and building of the nest. It takes two to three days to complete. The female never goes directly to the nest but lands on a nearby perch, then drops down and approaches under cover. When leaving, she walks about a foot from the nest and flies directly up. Her route to and from the nest remains fairly constant throughout the breeding period.

The male stays away from the nest while the female is building. He remains in another area of the territory and may sing or join the female briefly as she collects nesting materials. The nests are very difficult to locate, even after one has watched the birds come and go many times.

Locating the Nest

WHERE TO LOOK In open brushy areas, or at the edges of fields or roads

WHEN TO LOOK In late spring or early summer, soon after females have paired with males

BEHAVIORAL CLUES TO NEST LOCATION:

1. Locate the area of the pair through the male's singing and then follow the movements of the female.

2. Be suspicious of any area where the female seems upset at your presence and is giving the Chewink-call. She may have been disturbed from the nest, but you will have to move quite far away before she will return to it.

Breeding

Eggs: 3–5. Grayish with overall brown spotting concentrated at larger end

Incubation: 12–14 days, by only the female

Nestling phase: 9–11 days

Fledgling phase: About a month

Broods: 1–2

Egg-Laying and Incubation

Eggs are laid one per day until the clutch is complete. Incubation starts with the laying of the last egg. The female does all incubation and is very reluctant to flush from the nest; you may get to within a few inches of her before she moves. If scared off the nest, some females do a distraction display, fluttering along the ground, calling, and with wings and tail spread and drooped.

The male rarely approaches the nest during incubation; rather he remains in other areas of the territory, feeding, keeping intruders out, and singing or calling. The pair seem to be in only loose contact with each other at this time, for the most part leading independent lives. The female leaves the nest to feed about once every half hour. She often frequents the same feeding spot for several days. The male may join her as she feeds but always leaves her well before she comes to the area of the nest. On returning to the nest, the female usually gives a few Chewink-calls and then drops down and approaches the nest out of sight. In some cases the female may call a great deal on seeing you near the nest, and the male may not show up at all.

On the last few days of incubation, the male may come to the nest with food in his bill. He stays only a few seconds and then leaves. This has been called "anticipatory feeding" and may be the male's way of finding out when the young have hatched.

Nestling Phase

The female broods the young much of the time for the first six to seven days of the nestling phase. During this period the male sings very little as he gathers food and brings it to the nest to feed the young. The fecal sacs are at first eaten by the parents, but within a few days they are all carried away. Once the female stops brooding, she takes on the greater share of feeding the young, and the male will again be seen singing conspicuously about the territory.

After the seventh or eighth day of the nestling phase, the young will leave the nest if disturbed, even though they cannot fly. They will then be fed by the parents away from the nest.

Fledgling Phase

The young are fed by the parents for about a month after leaving the nest. At first they stay close together in dense cover on the parents' territory. After about a week they can fly short distances and become slightly dispersed in dense cover. Later they perch in more exposed places and are easier to see. When fully independent, they leave the territory and usually feed in the company of other immature Towhees. Young birds are able to go onto other territories without being attacked.

Plumage

DISTINGUISHING THE SEXES The sexes are easily distinguished through plumage, since the male has a black head, back, wings, and tail, while the female is brown in those areas. The male is also the only one to give versions of Song, although both sexes may give Quiet-song.

DISTINGUISHING JUVENALS FROM ADULTS Juvenal birds are buff colored and streaked on the sides, back, and head with olive brown.

MOLTS The one yearly molt for all Towhees occurs early in the season, starting as soon as mid-July. Following this, first-year males can be distinguished from adult males by their brown rather than black primary wing feathers; first-year and adult females cannot be distinguished.

Seasonal Movement

In much of the country the Towhee is a resident, but in the most northern areas it migrates south for the winter. This occurs in September. Migration north occurs in March and April. It is believed that both first-year and older males arrive together. Females arrive sometimes as much as a week or more later.

Flock Behavior

On their wintering grounds, Towhees stay in loose flocks averaging fifteen to twenty-five birds. These birds range over an area of twenty to thirty acres. In the more northern areas, there is a greater percentage of males in these flocks, presumably because the females migrate farther south.

Towhee flocks often join Cardinal flocks. Other birds associated with them in winter are Chickadees, Winter Wrens, White-throated Sparrows, Field Sparrows, Song Sparrows, and Juncos. The most common calls of the Towhee at this time are the Chewink-call and the Seee-call.

Chipping Sparrow / *Spizella passerina*

A SURPRISING FEATURE OF THE CHIPPING SPARROW IS HOW COMMON IT is around suburban areas and yet how little it is known and appreciated. Its favorite place to build nests is in the small evergreen shrubs so often used to landscape office buildings, houses, and small town parks. From the time the male first arrives, he sings a great deal from prominent perches at the tops of small trees. If his Song were more musical, perhaps this species would be better known. Instead, the Song is an extended series of slightly musical "chips" given repeatedly and almost monotonously. It is similar to some of the calls of crickets. The Song is easily blocked out in your mind, but once you begin to be sensitive to it, you will hear it all the time as you drive around suburban areas.

Another marvelous feature of the birds is that, like the Field Sparrows, males tend to have distinct versions of Song that they rarely vary, thus enabling you to recognize individual males as they engage in territorial interactions. Territories are often only a half acre in size, making it easy to follow all of the birds' activities.

There is very little courtship when the female arrives, but once paired, the two copulate frequently and this is often seen. Nest-building is also conspicuous; the female makes repeated trips with grasses in her beak and is usually accompanied by the male. This is the best time to locate the nest, for she will not hesitate to lead you right to it. The nests are usually low to the ground and afford a good view of the eggs and nestlings as they mature.

BEHAVIOR CALENDAR

	TERRITORY	COURTSHIP	NEST-BUILDING	BREEDING	PLUMAGE	SEASONAL MOVEMENT	FLOCK BEHAVIOR
JANUARY							■
FEBRUARY							■
MARCH					■		
APRIL	■	■	■		■	■	
MAY	■	■	■	■			
JUNE	■	■	■	■			
JULY	■	■	■	■			
AUGUST	■		■	■			
SEPTEMBER				■	■		
OCTOBER					■	■	
NOVEMBER						■	■
DECEMBER							■

DISPLAY GUIDE

Visual Displays

Wing-Droop
Male or Female   *Sp Su F W*

Wings are lowered so that their tips are noticeably below the line of the tail. Feathers on the crest may be raised.

CALL None

CONTEXT Done by territorial birds toward intruders. Often makes other birds leave.

See Territory

Wing-Flutter
Female   *Sp Su*

While perched, bird rapidly flutters tips of wings.

CALL A series of high, sibilant notes

CONTEXT Done by female when receiving food from the male, in which case the tail is held down; and done by the female during copulation, in which case the tail is held up.

See Courtship, Breeding

Auditory Displays

Song
Male   *Sp Su*

An extended, rapid series of slightly musical "chips." Repeated regularly. Each male has its own pitch and speed of Song, enabling you to distinguish between neighboring birds.

CONTEXT Given by males from conspicuous perches from the start of territory formation into the breeding phase. A softer series of rapid "chips" is given by either sex as they approach the nest during breeding. *See* Territory, Breeding

Chip-Call

Male or Female   *Sp Su*

A sharp, short note given singly but repeated at irregular intervals. May be soft or loud.

CONTEXT Given loudly when in response to danger, such as your proximity to the nest; given softly as a signal between the pair, especially when they are coordinating activities near the nest. *See* Breeding

Rapid-Chip-Call

Male or Female   *Sp Su*

A rapid series of soft "chip"s. A quiet call only heard a few yards away. Given irregularly

CONTEXT Given by either bird as it approaches its mate. Often occurs near the nest

Fledgling Call

Male or Female   *Su*

A short burst of loud "chip"s, given repeatedly. Similar in sound to the fledgling call of Cardinals.

CONTEXT Given by young during fledgling phase as they beg for food. *See* Breeding

BEHAVIOR DESCRIPTIONS

Territory

Type: Feeding, mating, nesting
Size: ½–1½ acres
Main behavior: Song, Wing-droop, chases
Duration of defense: From arrival on the breeding ground until the start of the fledgling period of the last brood

The territorial behavior of Chipping Sparrows is easy to follow, for the birds' territories are small, usually located in open fields or suburban areas, and differences in Song enable you to distinguish individual males (see Display Guide). When several males have adjacent territories, interactions are frequent.

Just after the males arrive on the breeding ground, they begin to claim territories by singing throughout the day from various prominent perches. If an intruder appears, the territory owner will first fly near him and Wing-droop. Often this is enough to make the intruder leave. Persistent intruders may enter a territory and sing. Even though chased by the owner, he remains in the territory and continues to sing. Interactions such as these may continue for an hour or more, with the owner being silent all the while. Sometimes fights occur in which the two males rise together twenty to thirty feet and grapple in midair.

During the fledgling phase, especially of the last brood, territorial behavior is less pronounced, and parents with their young tend to roam widely.

Courtship

Main behavior: Copulation
Duration: From arrival on the breeding ground until the egg-laying phase

Females usually arrive on the breeding ground a week or more after the males. They join males on their territories and form pairs with seemingly little ceremony. Once paired, the two stay close together and share in all activities.

The only sign of courtship that has been reported is copulation. The female initiates copulation by doing Wing-flutter. The male, which is usually singing from perches nearby, approaches, hovers over her back, and then lands and copulates. After copulation, the female preens. Copulation takes place on perches or on the ground, often interrupting the female's feeding or gathering of nest material. It may even occur while the female has nest material in her beak. Sometimes it is quickly repeated as many as four times in a single minute. Copulation continues into the egg-laying phase and, although it can occur at any time of day, it is most common from mid- to late morning.

Nest-Building

Placement: On horizontal branch 3–10 feet off ground, maybe lower
Size: Inside diameter 2 inches; inside depth 1½ inches
Materials: Weed stems, grasses, rootlets, lined with hair

Nest-building starts soon after the female arrives. The first stage is for the male and female to fly about together and enter various shrubs and evergreens to look for suitable nesting sites. Once one is found, the female builds the nest. Most construction takes place in early to mid-morning. The female may go up to one hundred fifty yards to collect material but usually finds adequate supplies nearer the nest site. Trips to and from the nest are quick, frequent, and usually conspicuous. The nest is completed in three or four days. A good place to watch for nest-building activity is near the evergreen plantings of suburban buildings.

While the female is building the nest, the male either accompanies her on collecting trips, stays near the nest site and sings, or flies to her and mates.

Locating the Nest

WHERE TO LOOK Suburban areas that have scattered evergreen foundation plantings and landscaping

WHEN TO LOOK Early in the season, soon after the female arrives, and on into the season, for renestings are common

BEHAVIORAL CLUES TO NEST LOCATION:

1. Look in the area of singing territorial males.

2. Look for female making repeated trips with grasses in her beak.

3. Look for pair on the ground with female picking up bits of grasses; follow her to nest.

Breeding

Eggs: 3–4. Pale blue with blotches or dots at larger end
Incubation: 11–12 days, by female
Nestling phase: 7–10 days
Fledgling phase: 3–4 weeks
Broods: 2

Egg-Laying and Incubation

The female starts laying as soon as the nest is finished, and eggs are laid one each day until the clutch is complete. Incubation starts the day before the last egg is laid. During incubation, the female alternates periods on the nest (averaging fifteen minutes) with periods off the nest (averaging eight minutes). The male often approaches the nest with food for the female, which he gives to her on the nest or a slight distance away after she gets off the nest. When the male approaches the nest, he gives the Soft-chip or Rapid-chip call. The female occasionally Wing-flutters when she receives food from the male.

Both the male and female may approach the nest in a circuitous manner, landing a slight distance away, then hopping to the spot. They both leave the nest more directly.

Nestling Phase

The female broods the young for the first six or seven days of the nestling phase. After the second or third day, the young give a low "zee-zee-zee-zee" call when fed by the parents. By the sixth day, the young start to cower if disturbed at the nest; before that they show little reaction. Brooding progressively lessens over the six or seven days during which it occurs. While the female broods, the male feeds the female and the young almost all of their food. In later stages, both male and female feed the young. Fecal sacs are carried away by both parents. The smaller ones from the first few days are eaten.

Fledgling Phase

If the young are disturbed in the last few days of the nestling phase, they may leave the nest early and perch on nearby twigs and branches. After two days out of the nest, the young can fly a short distance. After four days they can fly well. They are fed by the parents outside the nest for three to four weeks. The family tends to stay together for the remainder of the summer. A second brood is common, and during this you are likely to see the parents feeding the young of the first brood, while doing all activities to prepare for the second brood, such as renewed singing by the male, nest-building by the female, and copulation.

Plumage

DISTINGUISHING THE SEXES Although individual birds may vary slightly in bill color and head pattern, there is no consistent way to distinguish the sexes through plumage. You must use a variety of behavioral clues, such as the fact that only the male sings, and only the female builds the nest, incubates, and broods.

DISTINGUISHING JUVENALS FROM ADULTS Juvenals have five black or brown streaks on their breasts. Breasts of adults are clear and unstreaked.

MOLTS Chipping Sparrows undergo two molts per year: a complete molt in fall and a partial one in spring. In winter, the adults' rusty cap and bright white eye stripe are replaced by a tan eye stripe and dull, streaked cap.

Seasonal Movement

Chipping Sparrows migrate south from late September until early November. They tend to travel in flocks of about thirty birds, moving slightly as they feed during the day and migrating long distances at night. They spend the winter on the southern U.S. coast.

Chipping Sparrows generally fly north in April; but even as early as March, males may be heard singing on their territories. Spring migrants form small flocks of two to six birds.

Flock Behavior

Chipping Sparrows remain in flocks during the winter. A characteristic of these flocks is frequent midair fights accompanied by excited calls. The fights are short but occur so often that one can identify a flock of this species from other sparrows by the presence of the fights.

Field Sparrow / *Spizella pusilla*

FIELD SPARROWS ARE EXCELLENT BIRDS FOR BEHAVIOR-WATCHING. AS the name implies, their favorite habitat is old fields, where areas of uncut grass mix with vigorous sapling shrubs. One of the nicest features of the birds is the Song of the male, which is a long series of slurred whistles whose rhythm has been likened to the bouncing of a ping pong ball on a table: it gradually increases in speed. Each male has its own fixed version of this Song, and the versions are distinct enough that with a little listening you can come to recognize individuals quite easily by sound alone. The males also give Song frequently and loudly from exposed perches around their territory, so it is also not hard to get a sense of their territorial boundaries. The territories are only a few acres large and are often grouped together, so you can easily follow the birds and watch the males as they interact. The birds are often oblivious to your presence, which enables you to observe them from within a few feet.

When the females arrive and the males' singing rate markedly decreases, pairs form with relatively little display. Copulation is frequent and can be detected by hearing the Chip-call and Trill-call. During this stage and before nest-building has begun, the female may pick up and drop bits of grasses; when nest-building actually begins, she gathers clumps of material and flies directly to the nest. If you come anywhere near the nest during incubation or the nestling phase, the parents will chip excitedly in alarm. If you are patient and retreat a bit, they will resume their activities and you will discover the location of the nest. Fledglings actively follow the parents about. In late summer and fall the birds form large flocks in much the same habitats, and they feed and roost together until it is time to migrate.

BEHAVIOR CALENDAR

	TERRITORY	COURTSHIP	NEST-BUILDING	BREEDING	PLUMAGE	SEASONAL MOVEMENT	FLOCK BEHAVIOR
JANUARY							
FEBRUARY							
MARCH	■	■				■	
APRIL	■	■	■	■		■	
MAY	■	■	■	■			
JUNE	■	■	■	■			
JULY	■	■		■			
AUGUST					■		
SEPTEMBER					■	■	
OCTOBER						■	
NOVEMBER							
DECEMBER							

DISPLAY GUIDE

Visual Displays

Crest-Raise
Male or Female   *Sp Su F W*
Bird raises crest.
CALL Chip-call
CONTEXT Given in moments of alarm

Auditory Displays

Song
Male   *Sp Su*
A series of sweet, slurred notes, starting   *tewtewtew-*
slowly and gradually speeding to a trill. Pitch   *tewtewtew*
may rise or drop or stay the same. Each male
has a distinct variation of Song.
CONTEXT Given by males during territory
formation and courtship. *See* Territory,
Courtship

Chip-Call
Male or Female   *Sp Su F W*
A short, harsh sound, often irregularly
repeated
CONTEXT Given during territorial encoun-
ters, in situations of alarm, and at times
between members of a pair. *See* Territory,
Courtship

Trill-Call
Male or Female   *Sp Su*
An unvarying rapid series of high-pitched
notes. May be preceded by Chip-call

CONTEXT Given in territorial encounters and during copulation. *See* Territory, Courtship

Seee-Call
Male or Female   *Sp Su*
A soft, sweet, single note
CONTEXT Given between members of a pair when they are in close contact. *See* Courtship

Fledgling-Call
Male or Female   *Sp Su*
A short, buzzy note, often repeated
CONTEXT Given by fledglings when they are hungry

BEHAVIOR DESCRIPTIONS

Territory

Type: Mating, nesting, feeding
Size: 2–6 acres
Main behavior: Song, Chip-call, Trill-call, chases
Duration of defense: From arrival on breeding ground until fledging of last brood

Males arrive first on the breeding ground and immediately begin to set up territories by singing from prominent perches. Each male has his own version of Song, and, by listening carefully, you can begin to recognize individuals. In good habitats, territories can be quite small and have common borders. This enables you to see numerous interactions as returning males try to expand their old territories and new males try to claim one.

Territorial behavior includes singing from exposed perches and chases between neighbors. Chases usually occur within shrubbery and are accompanied by the Chip-call and Trill-call. Sometimes chases end in encounters in which both birds grapple on the ground. By listening for the Trill-call and approaching quietly, you can often get to within a few feet of competing males.

Both males and females have a strong tendency to return to the area in which they bred the previous season. If the exact territory they used the previous season is already occupied, they may compete for it or settle nearby.

Courtship

Main behavior: Brief period of chases, copulation, Seee-call, Trill-call
Duration: Pairing occurs in a day, copulatory behavior may continue for a week or more before each brood

If you return to an area where you have been observing an actively territorial male and find it surprisingly quiet, this may indicate that a female has arrived and paired with the male, since before pairing, males sing almost constantly, but once paired they reduce their singing substantially.

When a female first arrives on a territory, the male may fly at her and chase her as if she were an intruding male. If she does not flee, but persists on the territory, the male may accept her within a couple of hours. Once paired, the two move about the territory feeding and staying close together. The only sound they give is the soft Seee-call, possibly used as a contact note.

You may hear some Chip-calls and Trill-calls coming from among bushes. If you approach, you are likely to see the female fluttering her wings as she gives a soft Trill-call and the male nearby giving the Chip-call and copulating with her. During copulation the female crouches down, raises her tail, and quivers her wings while the male flutters his wings as he mounts her. For a moment both birds give the Trill-call. After copulation, the male may leave to sing briefly from one of his favorite perches. These interactions at first sound and look like male-versus-male territorial encounters, but when you get close, they can be distinguished by the lack of chasing, the copulatory behavior, and the softer version of the Trill-call used between the pair.

For the rest of the breeding season, the male still occasionally sings and will chase out or fight with any males that come into his territory. It is fairly common when two males are fighting for one to leave the interaction and go off to copulate with his mate, which is usually nearby.

Nest-Building

Placement: In clumps of weeds or grass, or in or at the base of low bushy shrubs. Early nests are placed on the ground, later nests may be 4 or more feet high.
Size: Inside diameter 2 inches; inside depth 1½ inches
Materials: Coarse grasses and weeds lined with fine grasses and hair

The female chooses the site and builds the nest. The male stays close by, accompanying her on trips to gather material and giving the Chip-call to warn of possible danger. In the early morning, you may hear him sing slightly more than he did after initial pairing.

Most nest-building occurs in the morning. The female generally gathers material in clumps and may fly up to one hundred yards to collect it.

Field Sparrow nests seem to be frequently preyed upon, in which case the birds renest. They may build up to seven nests in a single season before raising a successful clutch. The outer portion of the nest is loosely woven and composed of larger, coarser material, while the inner part is made up of finer material more tightly woven. When the nest is in a tree, it is not woven around branches but is just placed there, and it may fall out in a storm. Nests take two to seven days to build; early nests can take longer.

Locating the Nest

WHERE TO LOOK In old, overgrown fields with shrubs and small trees

WHEN TO LOOK Early spring through summer

BEHAVIORAL CLUES TO NEST LOCATION:

1. Get some sense of Field Sparrow territory by listening to singing males, and walk around the territory, watching to see where the bird gets most excited and chips the most.

2. Look early in the morning (6–11 A.M.) for the female gathering nest material, with the male staying nearby, chipping. Female flies directly to the nest.

Breeding

Eggs: 3–5. Pale blue with varying amounts of brown or purple blotches
Incubation: 10–11 days, by female only
Nestling phase: 6–8 days
Fledgling phase: 3–4 weeks
Broods: 1–3

Egg-Laying and Incubation

The eggs are laid one each day until the clutch is complete. Eggs are laid early in the morning, and the female starts incubating around the time the last egg is laid. The female incubates about 70 percent of the daylight hours, regularly leaving the nest for six- to twenty-five-minute breaks. The male may feed her while she is on the nest, or he may come to her, give the Chip-call, and then accompany her as they both feed away from the nest.

Nestling Phase

During the first few days of the nestling phase, the female broods the young during the day, particularly during bad weather. She also remains on the nest at night throughout this phase. Both parents feed the young, more frequently the older they get. Both parents remove fecal sacs.

Fledgling Phase

The young leave the nest after six to eight days. At first they hop unsteadily out and remain nearby. The young give continual buzzy, chipping notes that sound similar to the calls of Field Crickets. Both parents feed the young frequently, and after about five days they can fly and follow the parents about. After the young are independent, they gather into small flocks that may contain up to twelve birds. These flocks remain in thick cover in the vicinity of the nesting areas and are not bothered by territorial males. In late summer, young and adults gather together in flocks and feed in favorite areas, until they move south.

Plumage

DISTINGUISHING THE SEXES Male and female Field Sparrows are identical in plumage, so only behavior will enable you to distinguish them. The male is the only one to give Song, and the female is the only one to build the nest and incubate.

DISTINGUISHING JUVENALS FROM ADULTS Juvenals have fine streaks on the upper breast, whereas adults have an unstreaked breast. MOLTS There is one complete molt per year, in August and September.

Seasonal Movement

Field Sparrows vary in their migration habits. Some are migrants while others may be residents throughout the year; others may migrate one year and not the next.

In late summer, the adults and young gather into large flocks that feed and roost together. Migration south occurs from mid-September to mid-October. They winter in the southern United States and often join flocks of other birds, such as Chipping Sparrows. Movement north in spring is in small flocks mixed with other Sparrow species, and occurs from March into April.

Checklist of Nests and Displays

Glossary

Bibliography

Checklist of Nests and Displays

THIS CHECKLIST FOR THE NESTS AND DISPLAYS OF THE BIRDS IN THIS volume is provided to help you keep track of the behavior you have seen and what you can look for in the future.

Killdeer
  Circling-flights
  Horizontal-run
  Collar-show
  Scraping
  Side-tilt
  Bobbing
  Kideah-calls
  Stutter-call
  Pup-pup-call
  Nest

Spotted Sandpiper
  Strutting
  Wing-flutter
  Back-ruffle
  Distraction display
  Songs
  Kerrwee-call
  Squeal-call
  Nest

Mourning Dove
  Perch-coo

Charging
Bow-coo
Flap-glide-flight
Wing-raise
Billing
Long-coo
Short-coo
Nest

Belted Kingfisher
  Crest-raise
  Head/tail-bob
  Rattle-call
  Nest

Downy Woodpecker
  Bill-waving
  Crest-raise
  Still-pose
  V-wing
  Fluttering-flight
  Teak-call
  Whinny-call
  Queek-queek-call

Drumming
Fledgling-calls
Nest

Eastern Phoebe
  Raised-crown
  Wing-flutter
  Flight-display
  Song
  Chirp-call
  T'keet-call
  Chatter-call
  Nest

Eastern Wood Pewee
  Song
  Dawn-song
  Chip-call
  Twitter-call
  Nest

Barn Swallow
  Song

Chit-chit-call
Whistle-call
Stutter-call
Nest

Tufted Titmouse
Head-forward
Wing-quiver
Crest-raise
Song
See-jwee-call
Jway-call
High-see-call
Tseep-call
Nest

White-Breasted
Nuthatch
Song-bow
Tail-fan-back-ruffle
Wing-spread
Song
Ank-call
Ip-call
Pheeoo-call
Fledgling-call
Nest

Marsh Wren
Song-flight
Fluff-out
Song
Chek-call
Nest

Brown Thrasher
Wing-flutter
Song

Smack-call
Teea-call
Nest

Wood Thrush
Wing/tail-flick
Spread
Crest-raise
Horizontal-fluff
Song
Bwubub-call
Bweebeeb-call
Eee-call
Fledgling-calls
Nest

Cedar Waxwing
Side-hop
Head-forward
Wing-rowing
Seeee-call
Bzee-call
Bzee-zee-call
Tseeah-call
Nest

Yellow Warbler
Circling
Gliding
Tail/wing-spread
Moth-flight
Song
Chip-call
Metallic-chip
Titi-call
Zeeep-call
Nest

Eastern Meadowlark
Bill-tilt
Tail/wing-flash
Jump-flight
Fluff-out
Song
Dzert-call
Chatter-call
Flight-song
Beeert-call
Nest

Brown-Headed Cowbird
Bill-tilt
Topple-over
Head-forward
Song
Whistle-call
Chatter-call
Cluck-call
Nest (eggs)

Northern Oriole
Bowing
Wing-droop
Song-flight
Song
Chatter-call
Weeet-call
Alarm-call
Fledgling-calls
Nest

Scarlet Tanager
Wing-flutter
Wing-droop-tail-up
Wing-droop

Song
Chip-burr-call
Chip-call
Sweee-call
Tseah-call
Nest

Northern Cardinal
  Tail-flick
  Head-forward
  Song-flight
  Lopsided-pose
  Song
  Chip-call
  Kwut-call
  Peetoo-call
  Fledgling-calls
  Nest

Rose-Breasted Grosbeak
  Crest-raise
  Song-flight
  Wing-droop-fluff
  Song
  Chink-call
  Eee-call
  Chrr-call
  Fledgling-calls
  Nest

Indigo Bunting
  Tail-flick
  Crest-raise
  Moth-flight
  Body-fluff
  Song
  Flight-song

Chip-call
Zeep-call
Nest

Rufous-Sided
Towhee
  Wing-raise
  Tail/wing-spread
  Song
  Chewink-call
  Quiet-song
  Seee-call
  Nest

Chipping Sparrow
  Wing-droop
  Wing-flutter
  Song
  Chip-call
  Rapid-chip-call
  Fledgling-call
  Nest

Field Sparrow
  Crest-raise
  Song
  Chip-call
  Trill-call
  Seee-call
  Fledgling-call
  Nest

Glossary

Bill-wipe — Bill is wiped across a branch during confrontations

Brood — The birds hatched from one clutch of eggs

Brooding — The act of sitting over the newly hatched young to keep them warm; done by the parents in the first few days of the nestling phase

Brood patch — A spot on the breast of an incubating bird where there are fewer feathers and an increased blood supply to help keep eggs warm during incubation

Call — An auditory display, generally simpler in structure than song

Clutch — A set of eggs for a single brood

Courtship — All behavior that involves the relationship between males and females in breeding condition

Display — A stereotyped movement or sound that a bird makes, and that, when used in certain situations, affects the behavior of other animals about the displaying bird

Fecal sac — A small mass of excrement, surrounded by a coating of mucus, which is excreted by a nestling and carried off or eaten by the parents

Fledgling — A young bird that has left the nest but is still dependent on its parents for some or all of its food

Home range — An area inhabited by a bird, but not necessarily defended against its own or other species

Incubation — The act of covering the eggs to keep them warm and further their development

Mate-feeding — The feeding of one adult member of a pair by the other; usually occurs only during the breeding season (sometimes called "courtship feeding")

Nestling — A hatched bird that remains in the nest and is cared for by the parents or other adults

Pair formation — The aspect of courtship that involves the pair's first encounters and their becoming committed to each other

Primary roost — A fixed location at which birds habitually gather during the inactive phase of their day

Range — An area regularly inhabited by a bird, but not consistently defended

Seasonal movement — Predictable large-scale movement of populations over the course of the year

Secondary roost — Like the primary roost, but used for a shorter period of time and during the active phase of the birds' day

Song — A complex auditory display that may be partially inherited and partially learned

Territory — Any defended area

Bibliography

General texts

Bent, A. C. et al. 1919–1968. *Life histories of North American birds.* 23 volumes. New York: Peter Smith and Dover.

Forbush, E. H. 1925–1929. *Birds of Massachusetts and other New England states.* 3 volumes. Boston: Mass. Dept. of Agriculture.

McElroy, Thomas P., Jr. 1975. *The new handbook of attracting birds.* New York: Alfred A. Knopf.

Pettingill, O. S., Jr. 1970. *Ornithology in laboratory and field.* Fourth edition. Minneapolis: Burgess Publishing Company.

Robbins, Chandler S., Bertel Bruun, and Herbert S. Zim. 1966. *Birds of North America.* New York: Golden Press.

Terres, J. K. 1980. *The Audubon Society encyclopedia of North American birds.* New York: Alfred A. Knopf.

Killdeer

Allen, A. A. 1932. The Killdeer. *Bird Lore* 34: 159–169.

Davis, E. 1943. Study of wild and hand reared Killdeers. *Wilson Bull.* 55: 223–233.

Deane, C. D. 1944. The broken-wing behavior of the Killdeer. *Auk* 61: 243–247.

Furniss, O. C. 1933. Observations on the nesting of the Killdeer plover in the Prince Albert District in central Saskatchewan. *Can. Field-Nat.* 47: 135–138.

Hiett, L. D., and F. R. Flickinger. 1929. Speaking of Killdeer. *Bird Lore* 31: 319–323.

Lenington, S., and T. Mace. 1975. Mate-fidelity and nesting-site tenacity in the Killdeer. *Auk* 92: 149–151.

Lenington, S. 1980. Bi-parental care in Killdeer: an adaptive hypothesis. *Wilson Bull.* 92: 8–20.

Mace, T. R. 1978. Killdeer breeding densities. *Wilson Bull.* 90: 442–443.

Nickell, W. P. 1943. Observations on the nesting of the Killdeer. *Wilson Bull.* 55: 23–28.

Phillips, R. E. 1972. Sexual and agonistic behavior in the Killdeer. *Ani. Behav.* 20: 1–9.

Pickwell, G. 1930. The sex of the incubating Killdeer. *Auk* 47: 499–506.

——— . 1925. The nesting of the Killdeer. *Auk* 42: 485–496.

Simmons, K. E. L. 1953. Some aspects of the aggressive behavior of three closely related plovers (Charadrius). *Ibis* 95: 115–127.

Spotted Sandpiper

Gochfeld, M. 1971. Notes on a nocturnal roost of Spotted Sandpipers in Trinidad, West Indies. *Auk* 88: 167–168.

Hays, H. 1972. Polyandry in the Spotted Sandpiper. *Living Bird* 11: 43–57.

Knowles, E. H. M. 1942. Nesting habits of the Spotted Sandpiper. *Auk* 59: 583–584.

Knudson, M. L. 1972. Functional analysis of song in the Spotted Sandpiper. *Actitis macularia*. Master's thesis, U. of N. Dakota.

Miller, J. R., and J. T. Miller. 1948. Nesting of the Spotted Sandpiper at Detroit, Michigan. *Auk* 65: 558–567.

Mousley, H. 1920. The diving habits and community spirit of the Spotted Sandpiper. *Can. Field-Nat.* 34: 96–97.

———. 1937. Nesting habits of the Spotted Sandpiper. *Auk* 54: 445–451.

———. 1939. Nesting behavior of Wilson's Snipe and Spotted Sandpiper. *Auk* 56: 129–133.

Nelson, T. 1930. Growth rate of the Spotted Sandpiper chick with notes on nesting habits. *Bird-Banding* 1: 1–13.

Nichols, J. T. 1920. Limicoline voices. *Auk* 37: 519–540.

Oring, L. W., and M. L. Knudson. 1972. Monogamy and polyandry in the Spotted Sandpiper. *Living Bird* 11: 59–73.

Preston, F. W. 1951. Egg-laying, incubation, and fledgling periods of the Spotted Sandpiper. *Wilson Bull.* 63: 43–44.

Stevenson, H. M., Jr. 1944. Southeastern limits of the Spotted Sandpiper's breeding range. *Auk* 61: 247–251.

van Rossen, A. J. 1925. Observations on the Spotted Sandpiper. *Auk* 42: 230–232.

Mourning Dove

Austin, O. L., Jr. 1951. The Mourning Dove on Cape Cod. *Bird-Banding* 22: 149–174.

Chambers, G. D., et al. 1962. Characteristics of wintering flocks of Mourning Doves in Missouri. *J. Wildl. Manage.* 26: 155–159.

Cowan, J. B. 1952. Life history and productivity of Mourning Doves in California. *California Fish and Game* 38: 505–521.

Goforth, W. R. 1971. The three-bird chase in Mourning Doves. *Wilson Bull.* 83: 419–424.

———, and T. S. Baskett. 1971. Social organization of penned Mourning Doves. *Auk* 88: 528–542.

Jackson, G. L., and T. S. Baskett. 1964. Perch-cooing and other aspects of the breeding behavior of Mourning Doves. *J. Wildl. Manage.* 28: 293–307.

LaPerriere, A. J., and A. O. Haugen. 1972. Some factors influencing calling activity of wild Mourning Doves. *J. Wildl. Manage.* 36: 1193–1199.

Leopold, A. S. 1943. Autumn feeding and flocking habits of the Mourning Dove in southern Missouri. *Wilson Bull.* 55: 151–154.

Nice, M. M. 1922. A study of the nesting of Mourning Doves. *Auk* 39: 457–474.

————. 1923. A study of the nesting of Mourning Doves. *Auk* 40: 37–58.

————. 1938. Notes on two nests of the eastern Mourning Dove. *Auk* 55: 95–97.

Sayre, M. W., et al. 1978. Reappraising factors affecting Mourning Dove perch-cooing. *J. Wildl. Manage.* 42: 884–889.

Belted Kingfisher

Bailey, W. L. 1920. The Kingfisher's home life. *Bird-Lore* 2: 76–80.

Carey, H. R. 1909. Remarks on the habits of the Kingfisher on the New Hampshire sea-coast. *Bird-Lore* 11: 161–164.

Cornwell, B. W. 1963. Observations on the breeding, biology, and behavior of a nesting population of Belted Kingfishers. *Condor* 65: 426–431.

Davis, W. J. 1980. The Belted Kingfisher: its ecology and territoriality. Master's Thesis. U. of Cincinnati.

————. 1982. Territory size in Megaceryle alcyon along a stream habitat. *Auk* 99: 353–362.

Hamas, M. J. 1974. Human incursion and nesting sites of the Belted Kingfisher. *Auk* 91: 835–836.

Kilham, L. 1974. Biology of young Belted Kingfishers. *Am. Mid. Nat.* 92: 245–247.

Lincoln, F. C. 1924. A "territory" note on the Belted Kingfisher. *Wilson Bull.* 36: 113–115.

Mousley, W. H. 1938. A study of the home life of the Eastern Belted Kingfisher. *Wilson Bull.* 50: 3–12.

Skutch, A. F. 1957. Life history of the Amazon Kingfisher. *Condor* 59: 217–229.

White, H. C. 1953. The Eastern Belted Kingfisher in the maritime provinces. *Fisheries Res. Board of Canada Bull.* no. 97. 44 pp.

Downy Woodpecker

Haartman, L. V. 1957. Adaptations in hole-nesting birds. *Evolution* 11: 339–348.

Jackson, J. A. 1970. A quantitative study of the foraging ecology of Downy Woodpeckers. *Ecology* 51: 318–323.

Jackson, J. A., and E. E. Hoover. 1975. A potentially harmful effect of suet on Woodpeckers. *Bird-Banding* 46: 131–134.

Kilham, L. 1962. Reproductive behavior of Downy Woodpeckers. *Condor* 64: 126–133.

————. 1970. Feeding behavior of Downy Woodpeckers. I. Preference for paper birches and sexual differences. *Auk* 87: 544–556.

————. 1974. Play in Hairy, Downy, and other woodpeckers. *Wilson Bull.* 86: 35–42.

————. 1974. Copulatory behavior of Downy Woodpeckers. *Wilson Bull.* 86: 23–24.

————. 1974. Early breeding season behavior of Downy Woodpeckers. *Wilson Bull.* 86: 407–418.

Lawrence, L. de K. 1967. Comparative Life-history of four species of woodpeckers. *Ornith. Monogr.* no. 5.

Eastern Phoebe

Henderson, H. N. 1924. The Phoebe. *Bird-Lore* 26: 89–94.

Klaas, E. E. 1975. Cowbird parasitism and nesting success in the Eastern Phoebe. *Occ. Pap. Univ. of Kansas Mus. Nat. Hist.* 41: 1–18.

Middleton, D. S., and B. J. Johnston. 1956. The Mich. Audubon Soc. Phoebe Study — Part I. *Jack Pine Warbler* 34: 63–66.

Smith, W. J. 1969. Displays of *Sayornis phoebe*. *Behavior* 33: 283–322.

——. 1970. Song-like displays in Sayornis species. *Behavior* 37: 64–84.

——. 1970. Displays and message assortment in Sayornis species. *Behavior* 37: 85–112.

Smith, W. P. 1942. Nesting habits of the Eastern Phoebe. *Auk* 59: 410–417.

Stoner, D. 1939. Temperature, Growth, and other studies on the Eastern Phoebe. *N.Y. State Mus. Circ.* 22: 1–42.

Weeks, H. P., Jr. 1978. Clutch size variation in the Eastern Phoebe in southern Indiana. *Auk* 95: 656–666.

——. 1979. Nesting ecology of the Eastern Phoebe in southern Indiana. *Wilson Bull.* 91: 441–454.

Eastern Wood Pewee

Craig, W. 1926. The twilight song of the Wood Pewee. *Auk* 43: 150–152.

——. 1933. The music of the Wood Pewee's song and one of its laws. *Auk* 50: 174–178.

Elliott, A. 1909. Some nesting habits of the Wood Pewee. *Bird-Lore* 11: 154–157.

Gabrielson, I. N. 1922. Short notes on the life histories of various species of birds. *Wilson Bull.* 34: 193–210.

Rising, J. D., and F. W. Schueler. 1980. Identification and status of Wood Pewees from the Great Plains: What are sibling species? *Condor* 82: 301–308.

Barn Swallow

Davis, E. M. 1937. Observations on nesting Barn Swallows. *Bird-Banding* 8: 66–72.

Grzybowski, J. A. 1979. Responses of Barn Swallows to eggs, young, nests, and nest sites. *Condor* 81: 236–246.

Guillory, H. D., and D. J. LeBlanc. 1975. Mobbing and other interspecific aggression by Barn Swallows. *Wilson Bull.* 87: 110–112.

Hutton, A. E. 1978. Spatial relationships in perching barn and cliff swallows. *Wilson Bull.* 90: 396–403.

Jackson, J. A., and P. G. Burchfield. 1975. Nest-site selection of Barn Swallows in east-central Mississippi. *Am. Mid. Nat.* 94: 503–509.

Mason, E. A. 1953. Barn Swallow life history data based on banding records. *Bird-Banding* 24: 91–100.

Samuel, D. E. 1970. Banding, paint-marking, and subsequent movements of Barn and Cliff Swallows. *Bird-Banding* 41: 97–103.

——. 1971. Vocal repertoires of sympatric barn and cliff swallows. *Auk* 88: 839–855.

——. 1971. The breeding biology of Barn and Cliff Swallows in West Virginia. *Wilson Bull.* 83: 284–301.

——. 1971. Field methods for determining the sex of Barn Swallows. *Ohio J. Sci.* 71: 125–128.

Smith, W. P. 1933. Some observations of the nesting habits of the Barn Swallow. *Auk* 50: 414–419.

——. 1937. Further notes on the nesting of the Barn Swallow. *Auk* 54: 65–69.

Snapp, B. D. 1976. Colonial breeding in the Barn Swallow and its adaptive significance. *Condor* 78: 471–480.

Weeks, H. P. 1977. Nest reciprocity in Eastern Phoebes and Barn Swallows. *Wilson Bull.* 89: 632–635.

Wood, H. B. 1937. Observations at a Barn Swallow's nest. *Wilson Bull.* 49: 96–100.

Tufted Titmouse

Brackbill, H. 1949. Courtship feeding by the Carolina Chickadee and Tufted Titmouse. *Auk* 66: 290–292.

——. 1970. Tufted Titmouse breeding behavior. *Auk* 87: 522–536.

Condee, R. W. 1970. The winter territories of Tufted Titmice. *Wilson Bull.* 82: 177–183.

Dixon, K. L. 1949. Behavior of the Plain Titmouse. *Condor* 51: 110–135.

Eshbaugh, B. K. 1979. Removal of fur from a live raccoon by Tufted Titmice. *Wilson Bull.* 91: 328.

Gillespie, M. 1930. Behavior and local distribution of Tufted Titmice in winter and spring. *Bird-Banding* 1: 113–127.

Laskey, A. R. 1957. Some Tufted Titmouse life history. *Bird-Banding,* 28: 135–145.

Nice, M. M. 1933. Winter range of Tufted Titmice. *Wilson Bull.* 45: 87.

Offutt, G. C. 1965. Behavior of the Tufted Titmouse before and during the nesting season. *Wilson Bull.* 77: 382–387.

Short, M. 1933. Some Tufted Titmice life history. *Bird-Banding* 4: 159–160.

Sibley, C. G. 1955. Behavioral mimicry in the Titmice (Paridae) and certain other birds. *Wilson Bull.* 67: 128–132.

Van Tyne, J. 1948. Home range and duration of family ties in the Tufted Titmouse. *Wilson Bull.* 60: 121.

Wallace, G. O. 1967. An aggressive display by a Tufted Titmouse. *Wilson Bull.* 79: 118.

White-Breasted Nuthatch

Aldrich, J. W. 1944. Notes on the races of the White-breasted Nuthatch. *Auk* 61: 592–603.

Butts, W. K. 1931. A study of the Chickadee and White-breasted Nuthatch by means of marked individuals. Part III. *Bird-Banding* 2: 59–72.

Kilham, L. 1968. Reproductive behavior of White-breasted Nuthatches. (I. Distraction Display, Bill-Sweeping, and Nest Hole Defense.) *Auk* 85: 477–492.

——. 1971. Roosting Habits of White-breasted Nuthatches. *Condor* 73: 113–114.

——. 1972. Reproductive Behavior of White-breasted Nuthatches. (II. Courtship.) *Auk* 89: 115–129.

————. Covering of stores by White-breasted and Red-breasted Nuthatches. *Condor* 108–109.

————. 1981. Agonistic behavior of the White-breasted Nuthatch. *Wilson Bull.* 93: 271–274.

Tyler, W. M. 1916. A study of a White-breasted Nuthatch. *Wilson Bull.* 28: 18–25.

Marsh Wren

Kale, H. W., II. Eco. and Bioenergetics of Long-billed Marsh Wren in Georgia Salt Marshes. *Publ. Nuttall Ornith. Club,* no. 5.

Kroodsma, D. E., and J. Verner. 1978. Complex singing behaviors among *Cistothorus* wrens. *Auk* 95: 703–716.

Kroodsma, D. E. 1979. Vocal dueling among male Marsh Wrens: evidence for ritualized expressions of dominance/subordinance. *Auk* 96: 506–515.

Verner, J. 1963. Song rates and polygamy in the Long-billed Marsh Wren. *Proc. 13th Intern. Ornithol. Congr.,* pp. 299–307.

————. 1964. Evolution of polygamy in the Long-billed Marsh Wren. *Evolution* 18: 252–261.

————. 1965. Breeding biology of the Long-billed Marsh Wren. *Condor* 67: 6–30.

————. 1976. Complex song repertoire of male Long-billed Marsh Wrens in eastern Washington. *Living Bird* 14: 263–300.

Verner, J., and G. H. Engelsen. 1970. Territories, Multiple nest building and polygamy in the Long-billed Marsh Wren. *Auk* 87: 557–567.

Verner, J., and M. E. Wilson. 1966. The influence of habitats on mating systems of N.A. passerine birds. *Ecology* 47: 143–147.

Welter, W. A. 1935. The natural history of the Long-billed Marsh Wren. *Wilson Bull.* 47: 3–34.

Brown Thrasher

Erwin, W. G. 1935. Some nesting habits of the Brown Thrasher. *Jour. Tenn. Acad. Sci.* 10: 179–204.

Gabrielson, I. N. 1912. A study of the home life of the Brown Thrasher. *Wilson Bull.* 24: 64–95.

Perkins, S. E. 1930. The matings of the Brown Thrasher. *Wilson Bull.* 42: 221.

Sherman, A. R. 1912. The Brown Thrasher east and west. *Wilson Bull.* 24: 187–191.

Wood Thrush

Bertin, R. I. 1977. Breeding habitats of the Wood Thrush and Veery. *Condor* 79: 303–311.

Brackbill, H. 1943. A nesting study of the Wood Thrush. *Wilson Bull.* 55: 72–87.

————. 1948. A singing female Wood Thrush. *Wilson Bull.* 60: 98–102.

————. 1958. Nesting behavior of the Wood Thrush. *Wilson Bull.* 70: 70–89.

Dilzer, W. C. 1956. Hostile behavior and reproduction isolating mechanisms in the avian genera Catharus and Hylocichla. *Auk* 73: 313–353.

————. 1956. Adaptive modifications and ecological isolating mechanisms in the thrush genera *Catharus* and *Hylocichla*. *Wilson Bull.* 68: 171–199.

Longcore, J. R., and R. E. Jones. 1969. Reproductive success of the Wood Thrush in a Delaware woodlot. *Wilson Bull.* 81: 396–406.

Weaver, F. G. 1939. Studies in the life history of the Wood Thrush. *Bird-Banding* 10: 16–23.

Cedar Waxwing

Allen, A. A. 1930. The cherrybird—the Cedar Waxwing. *Bird-Lore* 32: 298–307.

Crouch, J. E. 1936. Nesting habits of the Cedar Waxwing. *Auk* 53: 1–8.

Gross, W. A. 1929. A Cedar Waxwing study in northern Michigan. *Bird-Lore* 31: 178–182.

Lea, R. B. 1942. A study of the nesting habits of the Cedar Waxwing. *Wilson Bull.* 54: 225–237.

Littlefield, M. J., and F. Lemkan. 1928. History of a Cedar Waxwing family. *Bull. Northeastern Bird-banding Assoc.* 4: 85–89; also 4: 73–76; 4: 77–85.

McCoy, H. 1927. A Waxwing ceremony. *Bird-Lore* 29: 188–189.

Nice, M. M. 1941. Observations on the behavior of a young Cedar Waxwing. *Condor* 43: 58–64.

Post, K. C. 1916. The Cedar Waxwing during July and August 1916. *Wilson Bull.* 28: 175–193.

Putnam, L. S. 1949. Life history of the Cedar Waxwing. *Wilson Bull.* 61: 141–182.

Saunders, A. A. 1911. A study of the nesting of the Cedar Waxwing. *Auk* 28: 323–329.

Whitman, F. N. 1919. A visit with Cedar Waxwings. *Bird-Lore* 21: 293–295.

Yellow Warbler

Bankwitz, K. G., and W. L. Thompson. 1979. Song characteristics of the Yellow Warbler. *Wilson Bull.* 91: 533–550.

Bigglestone, H. C. 1913. A study of the nesting behavior of the Yellow Warbler. *Wilson Bull.* 20: 49–67.

Clark, K. L., and R. J. Robertson. 1981. Cowbird parasitism and evolution of anti-parasite strategies in the Yellow Warbler. *Wilson Bull.* 93: 249–258.

Ficken, M. S., and R. W. Ficken. 1970. Responses of four warbler species to playback of their two song types. *Auk* 87: 296–304.

————. 1965. Territorial display as a population-regulating mechanism in the Yellow Warbler. *Auk* 82: 274–275.

————. 1965. Comparative ethology of the Chestnut-sided Warbler, Yellow Warbler, and American Redstart. *Wilson Bull.* 77: 363–375.

Kendeigh, S. C. 1945. Nesting behavior of Wood Warblers. *Wilson Bull.* 57: 145–164.

————. 1941. Birds of a prairie community. *Condor* 43: 165–174.

Morse, D. H. 1966. The context of songs in the Yellow Warbler. *Wilson Bull.* 78: 444–455.

Morton, E. S. 1976. The adaptive significance of dull coloration in Yellow Warblers. *Condor* 78: 423.

Mousley, H. 1926. Further study of the home life of the Northern Parula, and the Yellow Warbler and Ovenbird. *Auk* 43: 184–197.

Schrantz, F. G. 1943. Nest life of the Eastern Yellow Warbler. *Auk* 60: 367–387.

Smith, W. P. 1943. Some Yellow Warbler observations. *Bird-Banding* 14: 57–63.

Eastern Meadowlark

Lanyon, W. E. 1957. Comparative biology of the Meadowlarks in Wisconsin. *Publ. Nuttall Ornith. Club*, no. 1.

———. 1966. Hybridization in Meadowlarks. *Bull. Am. Mus. Nat. Hist.* 134: 1–26.

Nice, M. M. Displays and songs of a hand-raised Eastern Meadowlark. *Living Bird.*

Roseberry, J. L., and W. D. Klimstra. 1976. The nesting ecology and reproductive performance of the Eastern Meadowlark. *Wilson Bull.* 82: 243–267.

Brown-Headed Cowbird

Ankney, C. D., and D. M. Scott. 1982. On the mating systems of Brown-headed Cowbirds. *Wilson Bull.* 94: 260–268.

Burleigh, T. D. 1936. Egg-laying by the Cowbird during migration. *Wilson Bull.* 48: 13–16.

Darley, J. A. 1982. Territoriality and mating behavior of the male Brown-headed Cowbird. *Condor* 84: 15–21.

———. 1978. Pairing in captive Brown-headed Cowbirds. *Can. J. Zool.* 56: 2249–2252.

Dufty, A. M., Jr. 1982. Movements and activities of radio-tracked Brown-headed Cowbirds. *Auk* 99: 316–327.

Eastzer, D., P. R. Chu, and A. P. King. 1980. The young Cowbird: average or optimal nestling? *Condor* 82: 417–425.

Elliott, P. F. 1980. Evolution of promiscuity in the Brown-headed Cowbird. *Condor* 82: 138–141.

Friedmann, H. 1929. *The Cowbirds: A study in the biology of social parasitism.* Springfield, Illinois: Charles C. Thomas.

Krantz, P. E., and S. A. Gauthreaux, Jr. 1975. Solar radiation, light intensity, and roosting behavior in birds. *Wilson Bull.* 87: 91–95.

Laskey, A. R. 1950. Cowbird behavior. *Wilson Bull.* 62: 157–174.

Nice, M. M. 1949. The laying rhythm of Cowbirds. *Wilson Bull.* 61: 231–234.

Norman, R. F., and R. J. Robertson. 1975. Nest-searching behavior in the Brown-headed Cowbird. *Auk* 92: 610–611.

Payne, R. B. 1965. Clutch-size and numbers of eggs laid by the Brown-headed Cowbird. *Condor* 67: 157–174.

———. 1976. The clutch size and numbers of eggs of Brown-headed Cowbirds: effects of latitude and breeding season. *Condor* 78: 337–342.

Scott, D. M., and C. D. Ankney. 1981. Fecundity of the Brown-headed Cowbird in Southern Ontario. *Auk* 98: 677–683.

Northern Oriole

Beletsky, L. D. 1982. Vocal behavior of the Northern Oriole. *Wilson Bull.* 94: 372–381.

Erickson, J. E. 1969. Banding studies of Baltimore Orioles in North Carolina. *Bird-Banding* 40: 181-198.

Lawrence, R. E., and H. Brackbill. 1957. Winter returns of Baltimore Orioles in the Washington-Baltimore area. *Auk* 74: 261–262.

Miller, A. H. 1931. Notes on the song and territorial habits of Bullock's Oriole. *Wilson Bull.* 43: 102–108.

Nauman, E. D. 1930. The nesting habits of the Baltimore Oriole. *Wilson Bull.* 42: 295–296.

Pleasants, B. Y. 1979. Adaptive significance of the variable dispersion pattern of breeding Northern Orioles. *Condor* 81: 28–34.

Schaefer, V. H. 1976. Geographic variation in the placement and structure of Oriole nests. *Condor* 78: 443–448.

Schemske, D. W. 1975. Territoriality in a nectar feeding Northern Oriole in Costa Rica. *Auk* 92: 594–595.

Sealy, S. G. 1979. Prebasic molt of the Northern Oriole. *Can. J. Zool.* 57: 1473–1478.

——— . 1980. Reproductive responses of Northern Orioles to a changing food supply. *Can. J. Zool.* 58: 221–227.

Tyler, W. M. 1923. Courting Orioles and Blackbirds from the female bird's eye-view. *Auk* 40: 696–697.

Scarlet Tanager

Allen, A. A. 1932. The Tanager's story. *Bird-Lore* 34: 287–295.

Brecher, L. C. 1946. Notes on the nesting of the Scarlet Tanager. *Kentucky Warbler* 22: 46–50.

Ditcher, W. 1906. The Scarlet Tanager. *Bird-Lore* 8: 147–150.

Prescott, K. W. 1964. Constancy of incubation for the Scarlet Tanager. *Wilson Bull.* 76: 37–42.

——— . 1965. Studies in the life history of the Scarlet Tanager. *New Jersey State Mus.*, Investigations no. 2.

Northern Cardinal

Dow, D. D. 1976. Indexing population densities of the Cardinal with tape-recorded song. *Wilson Bull.* 82: 83–91.

Ganier, A. F. 1941. Through the seasons with the Cardinal. *Migrant* 12: 1–4.

Harvey, G. F. 1903. The diary of a Cardinal's nest. *Auk* 20: 54–57.

Laskey, A. R. 1944. A study of the Cardinal in Tennessee. *Wilson Bull.* 56: 27–44.

Lemon, R. E. 1905. The song repertoires of Cardinals at London, Ontario. *Can. J. Zool.* 43: 559–569.

——— . 1966. Geographic variation in the song of Cardinals. *Can J. Zool.* 44: 413–428.

——— . 1967. The response of Cardinals to songs of different dialects. *Anim. Behav.* 15: 538–545.

———. 1968. The displays and call notes of Cardinals. *Can. Zool.* 46: 141–151.

———. 1978. Relation between organization and function of song in Cardinals. *Behav.* 32: 158–178.

Lemon, R. E., and C. Chatfield. 1971. Organization of song in Cardinals. *Anim. Behav.* 19: 1–17.

Lemon, R. E., and A. Herzog. 1969. The vocal behavior of Cardinals and Pyrrhuloxias in Texas. *Condor* 71: 1–15.

Nice, M. M. 1927. Experiences with Cardinals at a feeding station in Oklahoma. *Condor* 29: 101–103.

Reese, J. G. 1975. Fall remex and rectrix molt in the Cardinal. *Bird-Banding* 46: 305–310.

Rice, O. O. 1969. Record of female Cardinals sharing nest. *Wilson Bull.* 81: 216.

Shaver, J. M., and M. B. Roberts. 1930. Some nesting habits of the Cardinal. *Journ. Tenn. Acad. Sci.* 5: 157–170.

———. 1933. A brief study of the courtship of the Eastern Cardinal. *Jour. Tennessee Acad. Sci.* 8: 116–123.

Rose-Breasted Grosbeak

Allen, F. H. 1916. The nesting of the Rose-breasted Grosbeak. *Auk* 33: 53–56.

Anderson, B. W., and R. J. Daugherty. 1974. Characteristics and reproductive biology of Grosbeaks in the hybrid zone in South Dakota. *Wilson Bull.* 86: 1–11.

Baird, J. 1964. Hostile displays of Rose-breasted Grosbeaks towards a red squirrel. *Wilson Bull.* 76: 286–289.

Dunham, D. W. 1966. Reaction to predators in the Rose-breasted Grosbeak. *Wilson Bull.* 78: 277–282.

———. 1966. Territorial and sexual behavior in the Rose-breasted Grosbeak. *Z. Tierpsychol.* 23: 438–451.

———. 1973. Agonistic behavior in captive Rose-breasted Grosbeaks. *Behavior* 27: 160–173.

Gabrielson, I. N. 1915. Field observations on the Rose-breasted Grosbeak. *Wilson Bull.* 27: 357–368.

Ivor, H. R. 1944. Bird study and semi-captive birds: the Rose-breasted Grosbeak. *Wilson Bull.* 56: 91–104.

Kroodsma, R. L. 1974. Hybridization in Grosbeaks (Phencticus) in North Dakota. *Wilson Bull.* 86: 230–236.

———. 1974. Species-recognition behavior of territorial male Rose-breasted Grosbeaks and Black-headed Grosbeaks. *Auk* 91: 54–64.

Lemon, R. E., and C. Chatfield. 1973. Organization of song of Rose-breasted Grosbeaks. *Anim. Behav.* 21: 28–44.

Rothstein, S. I. 1973. Extreme overlap between first and second nestings in Rose-breasted Grosbeaks. *Wilson Bull.* 85: 242–243.

Indigo Bunting

Allen, A. A. 1933. The indigo bunting. *Bird-Lore* 35: 227–235.

Bradley, H. L. 1948. A life history study of the Indigo Bunting. *Jack-Pine Warbler* 26: 103–113.

Cleveland, L. 1903. Nesting of the Indigo Bunting. *Bird-Lore* 5: 87–88.

Emlen, S. T. 1971. The role of song in individual recognition in the Indigo Bunting. *Z. Tierpsychol.* 28: 241–246.

Kohler, L. S. 1915. The Indigo Bunting in northern New Jersey. *Oologist* 32: 77–78.

Payne, R. B. 1981. Song learning and social interaction in Indigo Buntings. *Anim. Behav.* 29: 688–697.

Rice, J. O., and W. L. Thompson. 1968. Song development in the Indigo Bunting. *Anim. Behav.* 16: 462–469.

Sutton, G. M. 1959. The nesting Fringillids of the Edwin S. George Reserve, southeastern Michigan. *Jack-Pine Warbler* 37: 3–11.

Thompson, W. L. 1965. A comparative study of bird behavior. *Jack-Pine Warbler* 43: 110–117.

———. 1969. Song recognition by territorial male buntings. *Anim. Behav.* 17: 658–663.

———. 1970. Song variation in a population of Indigo Buntings. *Auk* 87: 58–71.

———. 1972. Singing behavior of the Indigo Bunting, *Paaserina cyanea. Z. Tierpsychol* 31: 39–59.

Rufous-Sided Towhee

Barbour, R. W. 1941. Winter habits of the Red-eyed Towhee in eastern Kentucky. *Am. Mid. Nat.* 26: 583–595.

———. 1951. Observations on the breeding habits of the Red-eyed Towhee. *Amer. Mid. Nat.* 45: 672–678.

Baumann, S. A. 1959. Breeding cycle of the Rufous-sided Towhee in Central California. *Wasmann Jour. Biol.* 17: 161–220.

Borror, D. J. 1975. Songs of the Rufous-sided Towhee. *Condor* 77: 183–195.

———. 1959. Variations in the Songs of the Rufous-sided Towhee. *Wilson Bull.* 71: 54–72.

Davis, J. 1958. Singing behavior and the gonad cycle of the Rufous-sided Towhee. *Condor* 60: 308–336.

———. 1960. Nesting behavior of the Rufous-sided Towhee in coastal California. *Condor* 62: 434–456.

Esten, S. R. 1925. Comparative nest life of the Towhee, Meadowlark, and Rose-breasted Grosbeak. *Proc. Indiana Acad. Sci.* 34: 397–401.

Gates, J. E., and D. M. Gates. 1975. Apparent brooding behavior of a male Rufous-sided Towhee. *Bird-Banding* 46: 253.

Heil, C. E. 1909. The Towhee. *Bird-Lore* 11: 158–160.

Kroodsma, D. E. 1971. Song variations and singing behavior in the Rufous-sided Towhee. *Condor* 73: 303–308.

Richards, D. G. 1979. Recognition of neighbors by associative learning in Rufous-sided Towhees. *Auk* 96: 688–693.

Roberts, J. B. 1969. Vocalizations of the Rufous-sided Towhee. *Condor* 71: 257–266.

Chipping Sparrow

Borror, D. J. 1959. Songs of the Chipping Sparrow. *Ohio Journ. Sci.* 59: 347–356.

Bradley, H. L. 1940. A few observations on the nesting of the Eastern Chipping Sparrow. *Jack-Pine Warbler* 18: 35–46.

Cottam, Clarence. 1933. Night migration of Eastern Chipping Sparrows. *Bird-Banding* 4: 54–55.

Dawson, W. R., and F. C. Evans. 1957. Relation of growth and development to temperature regulation in nestling Field and Chipping Sparrows. *Physiol. Zool.* 30: 315–327.

Marler, P., and D. Isaac. 1960. Physical analysis of a simple bird song as exemplified by the Chipping Sparrow. *Condor* 62: 124–135.

Walkinshaw, L. H. 1944. The Eastern Chipping Sparrow in Michigan. *Wilson Bull.* 56: 193–205.

―――. 1952. Chipping Sparrow notes. *Bird-Banding* 23: 101–108.

Field Sparrow

Best, L. B. 1977. Territory quality and mating success in the Field Sparrow. *Condor* 79: 192–204.

―――. 1977. Nestling biology of the Field Sparrow. *Auk* 94: 308–319.

―――. 1978. Field Sparrow reproductive success and nesting ecology. *Auk* 95: 9–22.

Crooks, M. P., and G. O. Hendrickson. 1953. Field Sparrow life history in central Iowa. *Iowa Bird Life* 23: 10–13.

Fretwell, S. D. 1968. Habitat distribution and survival in the Field Sparrow. *Bird-Banding* 34: 293–306.

Goldman, P. 1973. Song recognition by Field Sparrows. *Auk* 90: 106–113.

Heckenlively, D. B. 1976. Variation in cadence of Field Sparrow songs. *Wilson Bull.* 88: 588–602.

Laskey, A. R. 1934. Eastern Field Sparrow migration in Tennessee. *Bird-Banding* 5: 172–175.

Saunders, A. A. 1922. The song of the Field Sparrow. *Auk* 39: 386–399.

Walkinshaw, L. H. 1936. Notes on the Field Sparrow in Michigan. *Wilson Bull.* 48: 94–101.

―――. 1939. Nesting of the Field Sparrow and survival of the young. *Bird-Banding* 10: 107–114, 149–157.

―――. 1945. Field Sparrow, 39–54015. *Bird-Banding* 16: 1–14.